NEW LEFT REVIEW 71

SECOND SERIES

SEPT OCT 2011

PROGRAMME NOTES

WOLFGANG STREECK: Crises of Democratic Capitalism

The roots of today's Great Recession are usually located in the financial excesses of the 1990s. Wolfgang Streeck traces a much longer arc, from 1945 onwards, of tensions between the logic of markets and the wishes of voters—culminating, he argues, in the international tempest of debt that now threatens to submerge democratic accountability altogether beneath the storm-waves of capital.

DYLAN RILEY: Tony Judt—A Cooler Look

Few Anglophone intellectuals have received such posthumous acclaim as the Director of the Remarque Institute, leading contributor to the *New York Review of Books*, and late champion of social-democracy. Regularly compared to George Orwell, if not Isaiah Berlin, does any careful examination of his oeuvre sustain such panegyrics?

WILLIAM DAVIES: Political Economy of Unhappiness

As the bill for mental health problems—iconically, depression—climbs, economists seek to quantify the efficiency costs of unhappiness. In such quests, capitalism is reverting to classical psychologies of well-being, the better to neutralize the meaning of the new forms of illness—and its authorship of them.

MARK ELVIN: Multiple Revolutions

Beneath the dramatic social, political and military turmoil of China's last two centuries, Mark Elvin suggests, lay a series of existential crises amid the collapse of established pillars of authority, whose most vivid expression can be found in two largely forgotten novels of the 1920s and 1970s.

ANDY MERRIFIELD: Crowd Politics

From Joyce to Lefebvre, sign-posts to a morphology of the demonstration in the age of Twitter and Facebook. Is the city still the indispensable arena of any collective uprising, and what would it mean to claim a 'right' to it?

JACOB EMERY: Art of the Industrial Trace

Looking down at man-made landscapes from an airplane window: entry-point to an allegorical materialism, mapping art onto its double in production? The role of the indexical in earthworks, crop art and aerial photography, and the limits it places on allegory.

BOOK REVIEWS

PERRY ANDERSON on Patrick Wilcken, *Claude-Lévi-Strauss: The Poet in the Laboratory*. Deciphering the life and thought of the anthropological mage.

FREDRIC JAMESON on Uwe Tellkamp, *Der Turm*. Reunified Germany's best-seller from the former DDR, and the way time was lived in it.

STEVEN LUKES on John Hall, *Ernest Gellner: An Intellectual Biography*. Heterodoxies, philosophical and sociological, of England's outstanding post-war emigré.

CONTRIBUTORS

WILLIAM DAVIES: *at the Institute for Science, Innovation and Society, Oxford*

MARK ELVIN: *emeritus at* ANU *and Heidelberg;* Retreat of the Elephants *was published in 2004; see also* NLR *64, 52*

JACOB EMERY: *teaches Russian literature at Indiana University*

FREDRIC JAMESON: *most recent books:* Representing Capital *(2011)*, The Hegel Variations *(2010)*, Valences of the Dialectic *(2009); see also* NLR *56, 48, 55, 25, 23, 21, 4*

STEVEN LUKES: *author most recently of* Moral Relativism *(2009); a new edition of* The Curious Enlightenment of Professor Caritat *also appeared in 2009*

ANDY MERRIFIELD: *author of* Magical Marxism *(2011) and* The Wisdom of Donkeys *(2008); see also* NLR *6*

DYLAN RILEY: *teaches sociology at Berkeley; author of* The Civic Foundations of Fascism in Europe *(2010); see also* NLR *56, 48, 30*

WOLFGANG STREECK: *director of the Max Planck Institute for the Study of Societies, Cologne; most recent work,* Re-forming Capitalism *(2009)*

WOLFGANG STREECK

THE CRISES OF

DEMOCRATIC CAPITALISM

THE COLLAPSE OF the American financial system that occurred in 2008 has since turned into an economic and political crisis of global dimensions.[1] How should this world-shaking event be conceptualized? Mainstream economics has tended to conceive society as governed by a general tendency toward equilibrium, where crises and change are no more than temporary deviations from the steady state of a normally well-integrated system. A sociologist, however, is under no such compunction. Rather than construe our present affliction as a one-off disturbance to a fundamental condition of stability, I will consider the 'Great Recession'[2] and the subsequent near-collapse of public finances as a manifestation of a basic underlying tension in the political-economic configuration of advanced-capitalist societies; a tension which makes disequilibrium and instability the rule rather than the exception, and which has found expression in a historical succession of disturbances within the socio-economic order. More specifically, I will argue that the present crisis can only be fully understood in terms of the ongoing, inherently conflictual transformation of the social formation we call 'democratic capitalism'.

Democratic capitalism was fully established only after the Second World War and then only in the 'Western' parts of the world, North America and Western Europe. There it functioned extraordinarily well for the next two decades—so well, in fact, that this period of uninterrupted economic growth still dominates our ideas and expectations of what modern capitalism is, or could and should be. This is in spite of the fact that, in the light of the turbulence that followed, the quarter century immediately after the war should be recognizable as truly exceptional. Indeed I suggest that it is not the *trente glorieuses* but the series of crises which followed that represents the normal condition of democratic capitalism—a condition ruled by an endemic conflict between capitalist markets and democratic politics, which forcefully reasserted itself when high economic growth came to an end in the 1970s. In what follows I will first discuss the nature of that conflict and then turn to the sequence of political-economic disturbances that it produced, which both preceded and shaped the present global crisis.

I. MARKETS VERSUS VOTERS?

Suspicions that capitalism and democracy may not sit easily together are far from new. From the nineteenth century and well into the twentieth, the bourgeoisie and the political Right expressed fears that majority rule, inevitably implying the rule of the poor over the rich, would ultimately do away with private property and free markets. The rising working class and the political Left, for their part, warned that capitalists might ally themselves with the forces of reaction to abolish democracy, in order to protect themselves from being governed by a permanent majority dedicated to economic and social redistribution. I will not discuss the relative merits of the two positions, although history suggests that, at least in the industrialized world, the Left had more reason to fear the Right overthrowing democracy, in order to save capitalism, than the Right had to fear the Left abolishing capitalism for the sake of democracy. However that may be, in the years immediately after the Second World War there was a widely shared assumption that for capitalism to be compatible with democracy, it would have to be subjected to extensive political control—for example, nationalization of key firms and sectors, or workers' 'co-determination', as in Germany—in order to protect democracy itself from being restrained in the name of free markets. While Keynes and, to some extent, Kalecki and Polanyi carried the day, Hayek withdrew into temporary exile.

Since then, however, mainstream economics has become obsessed with the 'irresponsibility' of opportunistic politicians who cater to an economically uneducated electorate by interfering with otherwise efficient

---

[1] This paper was given as the 2011 Max Weber Lecture at the European University Institute, Florence. I am grateful to Daniel Mertens for his research assistance.
[2] For the term 'Great Recession', see Carmen Reinhart and Kenneth Rogoff, *This Time Is Different: Eight Centuries of Financial Folly*, Princeton 2009.

markets, in pursuit of objectives—such as full employment and social justice—that truly free markets would in the long run deliver anyway, but must fail to deliver when distorted by politics. Economic crises, according to standard theories of 'public choice', essentially stem from market-distorting political interventions for social objectives.[3] In this view, the right kind of intervention sets markets free from political interference; the wrong, market-distorting kind derives from an excess of democracy; more precisely, from democracy being carried over by irresponsible politicians into the economy, where it has no business. Not many today would go as far as Hayek, who in his later years advocated abolishing democracy as we know it in defence of economic freedom and civil liberty. Still, the *cantus firmus* of current neo-institutionalist economic theory is thoroughly Hayekian. To work properly, capitalism requires a rule-bound economic policy, with protection of markets and property rights constitutionally enshrined against discretionary political interference; independent regulatory authorities; central banks, firmly protected from electoral pressures; and international institutions, such as the European Commission or the European Court of Justice, that do not have to worry about popular re-election. Such theories studiously avoid the crucial question of how to get there from here, however; very likely because they have no answer, or at least none that can be made public.

There are various ways to conceptualize the underlying causes of the friction between capitalism and democracy. For present purposes, I will characterize democratic capitalism as a political economy ruled by two conflicting principles, or regimes, of resource allocation: one operating according to marginal productivity, or what is revealed as merit by a 'free play of market forces', and the other based on social need or entitlement, as certified by the collective choices of democratic politics. Under democratic capitalism, governments are theoretically required to honour both principles simultaneously, although substantively the two almost never align. In practice they may for a time neglect one in favour of the other, until they are punished by the consequences: governments that fail to attend to democratic claims for protection and redistribution risk losing their majority, while those that disregard the claims for compensation from the owners of productive resources, as expressed in the language of marginal productivity, cause economic dysfunctions that

---

[3] The classic statement is James Buchanan and Gordon Tullock, *The Calculus of Consent: Logical Foundations of Constitutional Democracy*, Ann Arbor, MI 1962.

will become increasingly unsustainable and thereby also undermine political support.

In the liberal utopia of standard economic theory, the tension in democratic capitalism between its two principles of allocation is overcome by turning the theory into what Marx would have called a material force. In this view, economics as 'scientific knowledge' teaches citizens and politicians that true justice is market justice, under which everybody is rewarded according to their contribution, rather than their needs redefined as rights. To the extent that economic theory became accepted as a social theory, it would 'come true' in the sense of being performative—thus revealing its essentially rhetorical nature as an instrument of social construction by persuasion. In the real world, however, it did not prove so easy to talk people out of their 'irrational' beliefs in social and political rights, as distinct from the law of the market and the right of property. To date, non-market notions of social justice have resisted efforts at economic rationalization, forceful as the latter may have become in the leaden age of advancing neoliberalism. People stubbornly refused to give up on the idea of a moral economy under which they have rights that take precedence over the outcomes of market exchanges.[4] In fact where they have a chance—as they inevitably do in a working democracy—they tend in one way or another to insist on the primacy of the social over the economic; on social commitments and obligations being protected from market pressures for 'flexibility'; and on society honouring human expectations of a life outside the dictatorship of ever-fluctuating 'market signals'. This is arguably what Polanyi described as a 'counter-movement' against the commodification of labour in *The Great Transformation*.

For the economic mainstream, disorders like inflation, public deficits and excessive private or public debt result from insufficient knowledge of the laws governing the economy as a wealth-creation machine, or from disregard of such laws in selfish pursuit of political power. By contrast, theories of political economy—to the extent that they take the political seriously and are not just functionalist efficiency theories—recognize

---

[4] See Edward Thompson, 'The Moral Economy of the English Crowd in the Eighteenth Century', *Past & Present*, vol. 50, no. 1, 1971; and James Scott, *The Moral Economy of the Peasant: Rebellion and Subsistence in Southeast Asia*, New Haven, CT 1976. The exact content of such rights obviously varies between different social and historical locations.

market allocation as just one type of political-economic regime, governed by the interests of those owning scarce productive resources and thus in a strong market position. An alternative regime, political allocation, is preferred by those with little economic weight but potentially extensive political power. From this perspective, standard economics is basically the theoretical exaltation of a political-economic social order serving those well-endowed with market power, in that it equates their interests with the general interest. It represents the distributional claims of the owners of productive capital as technical imperatives of good, in the sense of scientifically sound, economic management. For political economy, mainstream economics' account of dysfunctions in the economy as being the result of a cleavage between traditionalist principles of moral economy and rational-modern principles amounts to a tendentious misrepresentation, for it hides the fact that the 'economic' economy is *also* a moral economy, for those with commanding powers in the market.

In the language of mainstream economics, crises appear as punishment for governments failing to respect the natural laws that are the true governors of the economy. By contrast, a theory of political economy worth its name perceives crises as manifestations of the 'Kaleckian reactions' of the owners of productive resources to democratic politics penetrating into their exclusive domain, trying to prevent them from exploiting their market power to the fullest and thereby violating their expectations of being justly rewarded for their astute risk-taking.[5] Standard economic theory treats social structure and the distribution of interests

---

[5] In a seminal essay, Michał Kalecki identified the 'confidence' of investors as a crucial factor determining economic performance: 'Political Aspects of Full Employment', *Political Quarterly*, vol. 14, no. 4, 1943. Investor confidence, according to Kalecki, depends on the extent to which current profit expectations of capital owners are reliably sanctioned by the distribution of political power and the policies to which it gives rise. Economic dysfunctions—unemployment in Kalecki's case—ensue when business sees its profit expectations threatened by political interference. 'Wrong' policies in this sense result in a loss of business confidence, which in turn may result in what would amount to an investment strike of capital owners. Kalecki's perspective makes it possible to model a capitalist economy as an interactive game, as distinguished from a natural or machine-like mechanism. In this perspective, the point at which capitalists react adversely to non-market allocation by withdrawing investment need not be seen as fixed and mathematically predictable but may be negotiable. For example, it may be set by a historically changeable level of aspiration or by strategic calculation. This is why predictions based on universalistic, i.e., historically and culturally indifferent, economic models so often fail: they assume fixed parameters where in reality these are socially determined.

and power vested in it as exogenous, holding them constant and thereby making them both invisible and, for the purposes of economic 'science', naturally given. The only politics such a theory can envisage involves opportunistic or, at best, incompetent attempts to bend economic laws. Good economic policy is non-political by definition. The problem is that this view is not shared by the many for whom politics is a much-needed recourse against markets, whose unfettered operation interferes with what they happen to feel is right. Unless they are somehow persuaded to adopt neoclassical economics as a self-evident model of what social life is and should be, their political demands as democratically expressed will differ from the prescriptions of standard economic theory. The implication is that while an economy, if sufficiently conceptually disembedded, may be modelled as tending toward equilibrium, a political economy may not, unless it is devoid of democracy and run by a Platonic dictatorship of economist-kings. Capitalist politics, as will be seen, has done its best to lead us out of the desert of corrupt democratic opportunism into the promised land of self-regulating markets. Up to now, however, democratic resistance continues, and with it the dislocations in our market economies to which it continuously gives rise.

2. POST-WAR SETTLEMENTS

Post-war democratic capitalism underwent its first crisis in the decade following the late 1960s, when inflation began to rise rapidly throughout the Western world as declining economic growth made it difficult to sustain the political-economic peace formula between capital and labour that had ended domestic strife after the devastations of the Second World War. Essentially that formula entailed the organized working classes accepting capitalist markets and property rights in exchange for political democracy, which enabled them to achieve social security and a steadily rising standard of living. More than two decades of uninterrupted growth resulted in deeply rooted popular perceptions of continuous economic progress as a right of democratic citizenship—perceptions that translated into political expectations, which governments felt constrained to honour but were less and less able to, as growth began to slow.

The structure of the post-war settlement between labour and capital was fundamentally the same across the otherwise widely different countries where democratic capitalism had come to be instituted. It included an expanding welfare state, the right of workers to free collective bargaining and a political guarantee of full employment, underwritten by governments making extensive use of the Keynesian economic toolkit. When growth began to falter in the late 1960s, however, this combination became difficult to maintain. While free collective bargaining enabled workers through their unions to act on what had become firmly ingrained expectations of regular yearly wage increases, governments' commitment to full employment, together with a growing welfare state, protected unions from potential employment losses caused by wage settlements in excess of productivity growth. Government policy thus leveraged the bargaining power of trade unions beyond what a free labour market would have sustained. In the late 1960s this found expression in a worldwide wave of labour militancy, fuelled by a strong sense of political entitlement to a rising standard of living and unchecked by fear of unemployment.

In subsequent years governments all over the Western world faced the question of how to make trade unions moderate their members' wage demands without having to rescind the Keynesian promise of full employment. In countries where the institutional structure of the collective-bargaining system was not conducive to the negotiation of tripartite 'social pacts', most governments remained convinced throughout the 1970s that allowing unemployment to rise in order to contain real wage increases was too risky for their own survival, if not for the stability of capitalist democracy as such. Their only way out was an accommodating monetary policy which, while allowing free collective bargaining and full employment to continue to coexist, did so at the expense of raising the rate of inflation to levels that accelerated over time.

In its early stages, inflation was not much of a problem for workers represented by strong trade unions and politically powerful enough to achieve *de facto* wage indexation. Inflation comes primarily at the expense of creditors and holders of financial assets, groups that do not as a rule include workers, or at least did not do so in the 1960s and 1970s. This is why inflation can be described as a monetary reflection of distributional conflict between a working class, demanding both employment security and a higher share in their country's income, and a capitalist class striving to maximize the return on its capital. As the two sides act on mutually incompatible ideas of what is theirs by right, one emphasizing the entitlements of citizenship and the other those of property and market power, inflation may also be considered an expression of anomie in a society which, for structural reasons, cannot agree on common criteria of social justice. It was in this sense that the British sociologist, John Goldthorpe, suggested in the late 1970s that high inflation was ineradicable in a democratic-capitalist market economy that allowed workers and citizens to correct market outcomes through collective political action.[6]

For governments facing conflicting demands from workers and capital in a world of declining growth rates, an accommodating monetary policy was a convenient *ersatz* method for avoiding zero-sum social conflict. In the immediate post-war years, economic growth had provided governments struggling with incompatible concepts of economic justice with additional goods and services by which to defuse class antagonisms. Now governments had to make do with additional money, as yet uncovered by the real economy, as a way of pulling forward future resources into present consumption and distribution. This mode of conflict pacification, effective as it at first was, could not continue indefinitely. As Hayek never tired of pointing out, accelerating inflation is bound to give rise to ultimately unmanageable economic distortions in relative prices, in the relation between contingent and fixed incomes, and in what economists refer to as 'economic incentives'. In the end, by calling forth Kaleckian reactions from increasingly suspicious capital owners, inflation will produce unemployment, punishing the very workers whose interests it may initially have served. At this point at the latest, governments under democratic capitalism will come under pressure to cease accommodating redistributive wage settlements and restore monetary discipline.

3. LOW INFLATION, HIGHER UNEMPLOYMENT

Inflation was conquered after 1979 (Figure 1) when Paul Volcker, newly appointed by President Carter as chairman of the Federal Reserve Bank, raised interest rates to an unprecedented height, causing unemployment to jump to levels not seen since the Great Depression. The Volcker 'putsch' was sealed when President Reagan, said to have initially been afraid of the political fallout of Volcker's aggressive disinflation policies,

---

[6] John Goldthorpe, 'The Current Inflation: Towards a Sociological Account', in Fred Hirsch and Goldthorpe, eds, *The Political Economy of Inflation*, Cambridge, MA 1978.

FIGURE I. *Inflation Rates, 1970–2010*

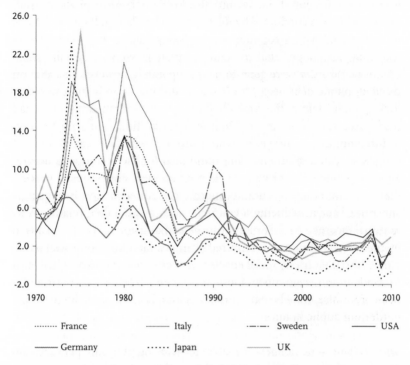

| France | Italy | Sweden | USA |
| Germany | Japan | UK | |

Source: OECD Economic Outlook Database No. 87

was re-elected in 1984. Thatcher, who had followed the American lead, had won a second term in 1983, also in spite of high unemployment and rapid de-industrialization caused, among other things, by a restrictive monetary policy. In both the US and the UK, disinflation was accompanied by determined attacks on trade unions by governments and employers, epitomized by Reagan's victory over the Air Traffic Controllers and Thatcher's breaking of the National Union of Mineworkers. In subsequent years, inflation rates throughout the capitalist world remained continuously low, while unemployment went more or less steadily up (Figure 2, overleaf). In parallel, unionization declined almost everywhere, and strikes became so infrequent that some countries ceased to keep strike statistics (Figure 3, overleaf).

The neoliberal era began with Anglo-American governments casting aside the received wisdom of post-war democratic capitalism, which held that unemployment would undermine political support, not just for the government of the day but also for democratic capitalism itself. The experiments conducted by Reagan and Thatcher on their electorates were observed with great attention by policy-makers worldwide. Those who may have hoped that the end of inflation would mean an end to economic disorder were soon to be disappointed, however. As inflation receded, public debt began to increase, and not entirely unexpectedly.[7] Rising public debt in the 1980s had many causes. Stagnant growth had made taxpayers more averse than ever to taxation; and with the end of inflation, automatic tax increases through what was called 'bracket creep' also came to an end. The same held for the continuous devaluation of public debt through weakening national currencies, a process that had first complemented economic growth, and then increasingly substituted for it, reducing a country's accumulated debt relative to its nominal income. On the expenditure side, rising unemployment, caused by monetary stabilization, required rising expenditures on social assistance. Also the various social entitlements created in the 1970s in return for trade-union wage moderation—as it were, deferred wages from the neo-corporatist era—began to mature and become due, increasingly burdening public finances.

With inflation no longer available for closing the gap between the demands of citizens and those of 'the markets', the burden of securing social peace fell on the state. Public debt turned out, for a while, to be a convenient functional equivalent of inflation. As with inflation, public debt made it possible to introduce resources into the distributional conflicts of the time that had not yet in fact been produced, enabling governments to draw on future resources in addition to those already on hand. As the struggle between market and social distribution moved from the labour market to the political arena, electoral pressure replaced trade-union demands. Instead of inflating the currency, governments began to borrow on an increasing scale to accommodate demands for benefits and services as a citizen's right, together with competing claims for incomes to reflect the judgement of the market and thereby help maximize the profitable use of productive resources. Low inflation was

---

[7] Already in the 1950s Anthony Downs had noted that in a democracy the demands from citizens for public services tended to exceed the supply of resources available to government; see for example, 'Why the Government Budget Is Too Small in a Democracy', *World Politics*, vol. 12, no. 4, 1960. See also James O'Connor, 'The Fiscal Crisis of the State', *Socialist Revolution*, vol. 1, nos 1 and 2, 1970.

FIGURE 2. *Unemployment Rates, 1970–2010*

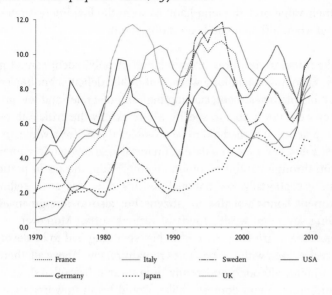

Source: OECD Economic Outlook Database No. 87

FIGURE 3. *Strike Days per 1,000 Employees, 1971–2007*

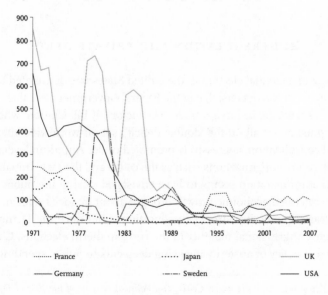

Source: Author's calculations of three-year moving averages based on ILO Labour Statistics Database and OECD Labour Force Statistics

helpful in this, since it assured creditors that government bonds would keep their value over the long haul; so were the low interest rates that followed when inflation had been stamped out.

Just like inflation, however, accumulation of public debt cannot go on forever. Economists had long warned of public deficit spending 'crowding out' private investment, causing high interest rates and low growth; but they were never able to specify where exactly the critical threshold was. In practice, it turned out to be possible, at least for a while, to keep interest rates low by deregulating financial markets while containing inflation through continued union-busting.[8] Still, the US in particular, with its exceptionally low national savings rate, was soon selling its government bonds not just to citizens but also to foreign investors, including sovereign wealth funds of various sorts.[9] Moreover, as debt burdens rose, a growing share of public spending had to be devoted to debt service, even with interest rates remaining low. Above all, there had to be a point, although apparently unknowable beforehand, at which creditors, foreign and domestic alike, would begin to worry about getting their money back. By then at the latest, pressures would begin to mount from 'financial markets' for consolidation of public budgets and a return to fiscal discipline.

4. DEREGULATION AND PRIVATE DEBT

The 1992 presidential election in the United States was dominated by the question of the two deficits: that of the Federal Government and that of the country as a whole, in foreign trade. The victory of Bill Clinton, who had campaigned above all on the 'double deficit', set off worldwide attempts at fiscal consolidation, aggressively promoted under American leadership by international organizations such as the OECD and the IMF. Initially the Clinton administration seems to have envisaged closing the public deficit by accelerated economic growth brought about by social reform, such as increased public investment in education.[10] But once the Democrats lost their Congressional majority in the 1994 midterm elections, Clinton turned to a policy of austerity involving deep cuts in public spending and

---

[8] Greta Krippner, *Capitalizing on Crisis: The Political Origins of the Rise of Finance*, Cambridge, MA 2011.
[9] David Spiro, *The Hidden Hand of American Hegemony: Petrodollar Recycling and International Markets*, Ithaca, NY 1999.
[10] Robert Reich, *Locked in the Cabinet*, New York 1997.

changes in social policy which, in the words of the President, were to put an end to 'welfare as we know it'. From 1998 to 2000, the US Federal Government for the first time in decades was running a budget surplus.

This is not to say, however, that the Clinton administration had somehow found a way of pacifying a democratic-capitalist political economy without recourse to additional, yet-to-be-produced economic resources. The Clinton strategy of social-conflict management drew heavily on the deregulation of the financial sector that had already started under Reagan and was now driven further than ever before.[11] Rapidly rising income inequality, caused by continuing de-unionization and sharp cuts in social spending, as well as the reduction in aggregate demand caused by fiscal consolidation, were counterbalanced by unprecedented new opportunities for citizens and firms to indebt themselves. The felicitous term, 'privatized Keynesianism', was coined to describe what was, in effect, the replacement of public with private debt.[12] Instead of the government borrowing money to fund equal access to decent housing, or the formation of marketable work skills, it was now individual citizens who, under a debt regime of extreme generosity, were allowed, and sometimes compelled, to take out loans at their own risk with which to pay for their education or their advancement to a less destitute urban neighbourhood.

The Clinton policy of fiscal consolidation and economic revitalization through financial deregulation had many beneficiaries. The rich were spared higher taxes, while those among them wise enough to move their interests into the financial sector made huge profits on the ever-more complicated 'financial services' which they now had an almost unlimited license to sell. But the poor also prospered, at least some of them and for a while. Subprime mortgages became a substitute, however illusory in the end, for the social policy that was simultaneously being scrapped, as well as for the wage increases that were no longer forthcoming at the lower end of a 'flexibilized' labour market. For African-Americans in particular, owning a home was not just the 'American dream' come true but also a much-needed substitute for the old-age pensions that many were unable to earn in the labour markets of the day and which they had no reason to expect from a government pledged to permanent austerity.

---

[11] Joseph Stiglitz, *The Roaring Nineties: A New History of the World's Most Prosperous Decade*, New York 2003.

[12] Colin Crouch, 'Privatised Keynesianism: An Unacknowledged Policy Regime', *British Journal of Politics and International Relations*, vol. 11, no. 3, 2009.

For a time, home ownership offered the middle class and even some of the poor an attractive opportunity to participate in the speculative craze that was making the rich so much richer in the 1990s and early 2000s—treacherous as that opportunity would later turn out to have been. As house prices escalated under rising demand from people who would, in normal circumstances, never have been able to buy a home, it became common practice to use the new financial instruments to extract part or all of one's home equity to finance the—rapidly rising—costs of the next generation's college education, or simply for personal consumption to offset stagnant or declining wages. Nor was it uncommon for home owners to use their new credit to buy a second or third dwelling, in the hope of cashing in on what was somehow expected to be an open-ended increase in the value of real estate. In this way, unlike the era of public debt when future resources were procured for present use by government borrowing, now such resources were made available by a myriad of individuals selling, in liberalized financial markets, commitments to pay a significant share of their expected future earnings to creditors, who in return provided them with the instant power to purchase whatever they liked.

Financial liberalization thus compensated for an era of fiscal consolidation and public austerity. Individual debt replaced public debt, and individual demand, constructed for high fees by a rapidly growing money-making industry, took the place of state-governed collective demand in supporting employment and profits in construction and other sectors (Figure 4). These dynamics accelerated after 2001, when the Federal Reserve switched to very low interest rates to prevent an economic slump and the return of high unemployment this implied. In addition to unprecedented profits in the financial sector, privatized Keynesianism sustained a booming economy that became the envy not least of European labour movements. In fact, Alan Greenspan's policy of easy money supporting the rapidly growing indebtedness of American society was held up as a model by European trade-union leaders, who noted with great excitement that, unlike the European Central Bank, the Federal Reserve was bound by law not just to provide monetary stability but also high levels of employment. All of this, of course, ended in 2008 when the international credit pyramid on which the prosperity of the late 1990s and early 2000s had rested suddenly collapsed.

FIGURE 4. *Fiscal Consolidation and Private Debt, as % of GDP 1995–2008*

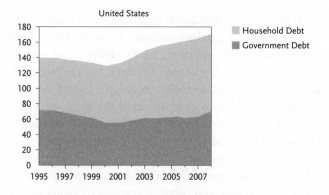

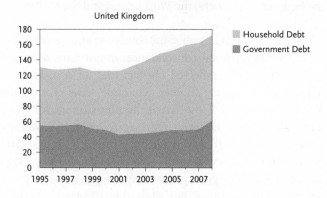

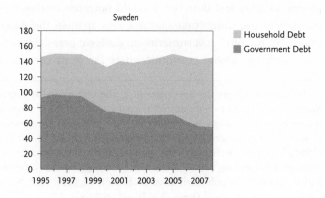

Source: OECD Economic Outlook Database No. 87, OECD National Accounts Database

5. SOVEREIGN INDEBTEDNESS

With the crash of privatized Keynesianism in 2008, the crisis of post-war democratic capitalism entered its fourth and latest stage, after the successive eras of inflation, public deficits and private indebtedness (Figure 5).[13] With the global financial system poised to disintegrate, nation-states sought to restore economic confidence by socializing the bad loans licensed in compensation for fiscal consolidation. Together with the fiscal expansion necessary to prevent a breakdown of the 'real economy', this resulted in a dramatic new increase in public deficits and public debt—a development that, it may be noted, was not at all due to frivolous overspending by opportunistic politicians or misconceived public institutions, as implied by theories of 'public choice' and the large institutional-economics literature produced in the 1990s under the auspices of, among others, the World Bank and the IMF.[14]

The quantum leap in public indebtedness after 2008, which completely undid whatever fiscal consolidation might have been achieved in the preceding decade, reflected the fact that no democratic state dared to impose on its society another economic crisis of the dimension of the Great Depression of the 1930s, as punishment for the excesses of a deregulated financial sector. Once again, political power was deployed to make future resources available for securing present social peace, in that states more or less voluntarily took upon themselves a significant share of the new debt originally created in the private sector, so as to reassure private-sector creditors. But while this effectively shored up the financial industry's money factories, quickly reinstating their extraordinary profits, salaries and bonuses, it could not prevent rising suspicions on the part of the same 'financial markets' that, in the process of rescuing them, national governments might have over-extended themselves. Even with the global economic crisis far from over, creditors began

---

[13] The diagram shows the development in the lead capitalist country, the United States, where the four stages unfold in ideal-typical fashion. For other countries it is necessary to make allowances reflecting their particular circumstances, including their position in the global political economy. In Germany, for example, public debt already began to rise sharply in the 1970s. This corresponds to the fact that German inflation was low long before Volcker, due to the independence of the Bundesbank and the monetarist policies it adopted as early as 1974; Fritz Scharpf, *Crisis and Choice in European Social Democracy*, Ithaca, NY 1991.

[14] For a representative collection see James Poterba and Jürgen von Hagen, eds, *Institutions, Politics and Fiscal Policy*, Chicago 1999.

FIGURE 5. *Four Crises of Democratic Capitalism in the US, 1970–2010*

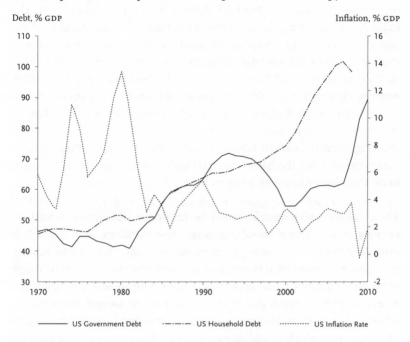

Debt, % GDP   Inflation, % GDP

——— US Government Debt   ·—·—·— US Household Debt   ··········· US Inflation Rate

Source: OECD Economic Outlook Database No. 87

vociferously to demand a return to sound money through fiscal auster-ity, in search for reassurance that their vastly increased investment in government debt would not be lost.

In the three years since 2008, distributional conflict under democratic capitalism has turned into a complicated tug-of-war between global finan-cial investors and sovereign nation-states. Where in the past workers struggled with employers, citizens with finance ministers, and private debtors with private banks, it is now financial institutions wrestling with the very states that they had only recently blackmailed into saving them. But the underlying configuration of power and interests is far more complex and still awaits systematic exploration. For example, since the crisis financial markets have returned to charging different states widely varying interest rates, thereby differentiating the pressure they apply on governments to make their citizens acquiesce in unprecedented spending cuts—in line, again, with a basically unmodified market logic of distribution. Given the amount of debt carried by most states today, even minor increases in the rate of interest on government bonds can cause fiscal disaster.[15] At the same time, markets must avoid pushing states into declaring sovereign bankruptcy, always an option for governments if market pressures become too strong. This is why other states have to be found that are willing to bail out those most at risk, in order to protect themselves from a general increase in interest rates on government bonds that the first default would cause. A similar type of 'solidarity' between states in the interest of investors is fostered where sovereign default would hit banks located outside the defaulting country, which might force the banks' home countries once again to nationalize huge amounts of bad debt in order to stabilize their economies.

There are still more ways in which the tension in democratic capitalism between demands for social rights and the workings of free markets expresses itself today. Some governments, including the Obama administration, have attempted to generate renewed economic growth through even more debt—in the hope that future consolidation policies will be assisted by a growth dividend. Others may be secretly hoping for a return to inflation, melting down accumulated debt by softly expropriating creditors—which would, like economic growth, mitigate the political tensions to be expected from austerity. At the same time, financial markets may be looking forward to a promising fight against political interference, once and for all reinstating market discipline and putting an end to all political attempts to subvert it.

Further complications arise from the fact that financial markets need government debt for safe investment; pressing too hard for balanced budgets may deprive them of highly desirable investment opportunities. The middle classes of the advanced-capitalist countries have put a good part of their savings into government bonds, while many workers are now heavily invested in supplementary pensions. Balanced budgets would likely involve states having to take from their middle classes, in the form of higher taxes, what these classes now save and invest, among other things in public debt. Not only would citizens no longer collect interest, but they would also cease to be able to pass their savings on

---

[15] For a state with public debt equalling 100 per cent of GDP, an increase by 2 percentage points in the average rate of interest it has to pay to its creditors would raise its yearly deficit by the same amount. A current budget deficit of 4 per cent of GDP would as a result increase by half.

to their children. However, while this should make them interested in states being, if not debt-free, then reliably able to fulfil their obligations to their creditors, it may also mean that they have to pay for their government's liquidity in the form of deep cuts in public benefits and services on which they also in part depend.

However complicated the cross-cutting cleavages in the emerging international politics of public debt, the price for financial stabilization is likely to be paid by those other than the owners of money, or at least of real money. For example, public-pension reform will be accelerated by fiscal pressures; and to the extent that governments default anywhere in the world, private pensions will be hit as well. The average citizen will pay—for the consolidation of public finances, the bankruptcy of foreign states, the rising rates of interest on the public debt and, if necessary, for another rescue of national and international banks—with his or her private savings, cuts in public entitlements, reduced public services and higher taxation.

6. SEQUENTIAL DISPLACEMENTS

In the four decades since the end of post-war growth, the epicentre of the tectonic tension within democratic capitalism has migrated from one institutional location to the next, giving rise to a sequence of different but systematically related economic disturbances. In the 1970s the conflict between democratic claims for social justice and capitalist demands for distribution by marginal productivity, or 'economic justice', played itself out primarily in national labour markets, where trade-union wage pressure under politically guaranteed full employment caused accelerating inflation. When what was, in effect, redistribution by debasement of the currency became economically unsustainable, forcing governments to put an end to it at high political risk, the conflict re-emerged in the electoral arena. Here it gave rise to growing disparity between public spending and public revenues and, as a consequence, to rapidly rising public debt, in response to voter demands for benefits and services in excess of what a democratic-capitalist economy could be made to hand over to its 'tax state'.[16]

---

[16] Joseph Schumpeter, 'The Crisis of the Tax State' [1918], in Richard Swedberg, ed., *The Economics and Sociology of Capitalism*, Princeton, NJ 1991.

When efforts to rein in public debt became unavoidable, however, they had to be accompanied for the sake of social peace by financial deregulation, easing access to private credit, as an alternative route to accommodating normatively and politically powerful demands of citizens for security and prosperity. This, too, lasted not much longer than a decade until the global economy almost faltered under the burden of unrealistic promises of future payment for present consumption and investment, licensed by governments in compensation for fiscal austerity. Since then, the clash between popular ideas of social justice and economic insistence on market justice has once again changed sites, re-emerging this time in international capital markets and the complex contests currently taking place between financial institutions and electorates, governments, states and international organizations. Now the issue is how far states can go in imposing the property rights and profit expectations of the markets on their citizens, while avoiding having to declare bankruptcy and protecting what may still remain of their democratic legitimacy.

Toleration of inflation, acceptance of public debt and deregulation of private credit were no more than temporary stopgaps for governments confronted with an apparently irrepressible conflict between the two contradictory principles of allocation under democratic capitalism: social rights on the one hand and marginal productivity, as evaluated by the market, on the other. Each of the three worked for a while, but then began to cause more problems than they solved, indicating that a lasting reconciliation between social and economic stability in capitalist democracies is a utopian project. All that governments were able to achieve in dealing with the crises of their day was to move them to new arenas, where they reappeared in new forms. There is no reason to believe that this process—the successive manifestation of democratic capitalism's contradictions, in ever new varieties of economic disorder— should have ended.

7. POLITICAL DISORDER

At this point, it seems clear that the political manageability of democratic capitalism has sharply declined in recent years, more in some countries than in others, but also overall, in the emerging global political-economic system. As a result the risks seem to be growing, both for democracy and for the economy. Since the Great Depression policy-makers have rarely, if ever, been faced with as much uncertainty as today. One example among many is that the markets expect not just fiscal consolidation but also, and at the same time, a reasonable prospect of future economic growth. How the two may be combined is not at all clear. Although the risk premium on Irish government debt fell when the country pledged itself to aggressive deficit reduction, a few weeks later it rose again, allegedly because the country's consolidation programme appeared so strict that it would make economic recovery impossible.[17] Moreover, there is a widely shared conviction that the next bubble is already building somewhere in a world that is more than ever flooded with cheap money. Subprime mortgages may no longer offer themselves for investment, at least not for the time being. But there are the markets for raw materials, or the new internet economy. Nothing prevents financial firms from using the surplus of money provided by the central banks to enter whatever appear to be the new growth sectors, on behalf of their favourite clients and, of course, themselves. After all, with regulatory reform in the financial sector having failed in almost all respects, capital requirements are little higher than they were, and the banks that were too big to fail in 2008 can count on being so also in 2012 or 2013. This leaves them with the same capacity for blackmailing the public that they were able to deploy so skilfully three years ago. But now the public bailout of private capitalism on the model of 2008 may be impossible to repeat, if only because public finances are already stretched to the limit.

Yet democracy is as much at risk as the economy in the current crisis, if not more. Not only has the 'system integration' of contemporary societies—that is, the efficient functioning of their capitalist economies—become precarious, but so has their 'social integration'.[18] With the arrival of a new age of austerity, the capacity of national states to mediate between the rights of citizens and the requirements of capital accumulation has been severely affected. Governments everywhere face stronger resistance to tax increases, particularly in highly indebted countries where

---

[17] In other words, not even 'the markets' are willing to put their money on the supply-side mantra according to which growth is stimulated by cuts in public spending. On the other hand, who can say how much new debt is enough, and how much too much, for a country to outgrow its old debt.

[18] The concepts were laid out by David Lockwood in 'Social Integration and System Integration', in George Zollschan and Walter Hirsch, eds, *Explorations in Social Change*, London 1964.

fresh public money will have to be spent for many years to pay for goods that have long been consumed. Moreover, with ever-tighter global interdependence, it is no longer possible to pretend that the tensions between economy and society, between capitalism and democracy, can be handled inside national political communities. No government today can govern without paying close attention to international constraints and obligations, including those of the financial markets forcing the state to impose sacrifices on its population. The crises and contradictions of democratic capitalism have finally become internationalized, playing themselves out not just within states but also between them, in combinations and permutations as yet unexplored.

As we now read almost every day in the papers, 'the markets' have begun to dictate in unprecedented ways what presumably sovereign and democratic states may still do for their citizens and what they must refuse them. The same Manhattan-based ratings agencies that were instrumental in bringing about the disaster of the global money industry are now threatening to downgrade the bonds of states that accepted a previously unimaginable level of new debt to rescue that industry and the capitalist economy as a whole. Politics still contains and distorts markets, but only, it seems, at a level far remote from the daily experience and organizational capacities of normal people: the US, armed to the teeth not just with aircraft carriers but also with an unlimited supply of credit cards, still gets China to buy its mounting debt. All others have to listen to what 'the markets' tell them. As a result citizens increasingly perceive their governments, not as *their* agents, but as those of other states or of international organizations, such as the IMF or the European Union, immeasurably more insulated from electoral pressure than was the traditional nation-state. In countries like Greece and Ireland, anything resembling democracy will be effectively suspended for many years; in order to behave 'responsibly', as defined by international markets and institutions, national governments will have to impose strict austerity, at the price of becoming increasingly unresponsive to their citizens.[19]

Democracy is not just being pre-empted in those countries that are currently under attack by 'the markets'. Germany, which is still doing relatively well economically, has committed itself to decades of

---

[19] Peter Mair, 'Representative versus Responsible Government', Max Planck Institute for the Study of Societies Working Paper 09/8, Cologne 2009.

public-expenditure cuts. In addition, the German government will again have to get its citizens to provide liquidity to countries at risk of defaulting, not just to save German banks but also to stabilize the common European currency and prevent a general increase in the rate of interest on public debt, as is likely to occur in the case of the first country collapsing. The high political cost of this can be measured in the progressive decay of the Merkel government's electoral capital, resulting in a series of defeats in major regional elections over the past year. Populist rhetoric to the effect that perhaps creditors should also pay a share of the costs, as vented by the Chancellor in early 2010, was quickly abandoned when 'the markets' expressed shock by slightly raising the rate of interest on new public debt. Now the talk is about the need to shift, in the words of the German Finance Minister, from old-fashioned 'government', which is no longer up to the new challenges of globalization, to 'governance', meaning in particular a lasting curtailment of the budgetary authority of the Bundestag.[20]

The political expectations that democratic states are now facing from their new principals may be impossible to meet. International markets and institutions require that not just governments but also citizens credibly commit themselves to fiscal consolidation. Political parties that oppose austerity must be resoundingly defeated in national elections, and both government and opposition must be publicly pledged to 'sound finance', or else the cost of debt service will rise. Elections in which voters have no effective choice, however, may be perceived by them as inauthentic, which may cause all sorts of political disorder, from declining turnout to a rise of populist parties to riots in the streets.

One factor here is that the arenas of distributional conflict have become ever more remote from popular politics. The national labour markets of the 1970s, with the manifold opportunities they offered for corporatist political mobilization and inter-class coalitions, or the politics of public

---

[20] According to Wolfgang Schäuble: 'We need new forms of international governance, global governance and European governance.' *Financial Times*, 5 December 2010. Schäuble acknowledged that if the German parliament was asked to forfeit its jurisdiction over the budget immediately, 'you would not get a Yes vote'—'[but] if you would give us some months to work on this, and if you give us the hope that other member states will agree as well, I would see a chance.' Schäuble was, fittingly, speaking as winner of the FT competition for European finance minister of the year.

spending in the 1980s, were not necessarily beyond the grasp or the strategic reach of the 'man in the street'. Since then, the battlefields on which the contradictions of democratic capitalism are fought out have become ever more complex, making it exceedingly difficult for anyone outside the political and financial elites to recognize the underlying interests and identify their own.[21] While this may generate apathy at the mass level and thereby make life easier for the elites, there is no rely- ing on it, in a world in which blind compliance with financial investors is propounded as the only rational and responsible behaviour. To those who refuse to be talked out of other social rationalities and responsibili- ties, such a world may appear simply absurd—at which point the only rational and responsible conduct would be to throw as many wrenches as possible into the works of *haute finance*. Where democracy as we know it is effectively suspended, as it already is in countries like Greece, Ireland and Portugal, street riots and popular insurrection may be the last remaining mode of political expression for those devoid of market power. Should we hope in the name of democracy that we will soon have the opportunity to observe a few more examples?

Social science can do little, if anything, to help resolve the structural ten- sions and contradictions underlying the economic and social disorders of the day. What it can do, however, is bring them to light and identify the historical continuities in which present crises can be fully under- stood. It also can—and must—point out the drama of democratic states being turned into debt-collecting agencies on behalf of a global oligarchy of investors, compared to which C. Wright Mills's 'power elite' appears a

---

[21] For example, political appeals for redistributive 'solidarity' are now directed at entire nations asked by international organizations to support other entire nations, such as Slovenia being urged to help Ireland, Greece and Portugal. This hides the fact that those being supported by this sort of 'international solidarity' are not the people in the streets but the banks, domestic and foreign, that would other- wise have to accept losses, or lower profits. It also neglects differences in national income. While Germans are on average richer than Greeks (although some Greeks are much richer than almost all Germans), Slovenians are on average much poorer than the Irish, who have statistically a higher per capita income than nearly all Euro countries, including Germany. Essentially the new conflict alignment translates class conflicts into international conflicts, pitting against each other nations that are each subject to the same financial market pressures for public austerity. Ordinary people are told to demand 'sacrifices' from other ordinary people, who happen to be citizens of other states, rather than from those who have long resumed collecting their 'bonuses'.

shining example of liberal pluralism.[22] More than ever, economic power seems today to have become political power, while citizens appear to be almost entirely stripped of their democratic defences and their capacity to impress upon the political economy interests and demands that are incommensurable with those of capital owners. In fact, looking back at the democratic-capitalist crisis sequence since the 1970s, there seems a real possibility of a new, if temporary, settlement of social conflict in advanced capitalism, this time entirely in favour of the propertied classes now firmly entrenched in their politically unassailable stronghold, the international financial industry.

---

[22] C. Wright Mills, *The Power Elite*, Oxford 1956.

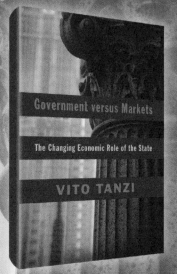

DYLAN RILEY

TONY JUDT:

A COOLER LOOK

ACCOLADES CONTINUE TO be piled upon the historian Tony Judt, following his untimely death in August 2010. For the *Guardian*, he was 'a fearless critic of narrow orthodoxies', 'a great historian', 'a brilliant political commentator'. For the *New York Review of Books*, 'a source of inspiration', who sought to 'embrace difference'—'like Isaiah Berlin'—within historical accounts that were 'harmonious, convincing, and true'; like Camus, Blum and Aron, Judt knew what it was to bear the intellectual's 'burden of responsibility'. To the *Economist*, he was 'erudite and far-sighted', 'a meticulous intellect'—'an intellectual with a capital I'. More circumspectly, the *New York Times* saluted his 'deep suspicion of left-wing ideologues'.[1] In June 2011 a Paris conference, jointly organized by the NYRB and CERI SciencesPo, celebrated Judt's 'scholarly rigour, elegance of style and acuteness of judgement'. Morally, he was 'fearless', 'prophetic', a new Orwell; intellectually, he was 'formidable', possessed of a 'forceful lucidity'; as a historian of French political life, happily 'inoculated against the revolutionary ideas that had been the stock in trade of the intellectual *engagé*.[2] To what extent are these plaudits confirmed by a sober examination of Judt's work, held to the normal scholarly standards of intellectual coherence and empirical plausibility? What follows will offer an evaluation of his writings, as the necessary precondition for an adequate assessment of his contribution as historian, publicist and scholar.

Tony Judt was born in 1948, the son of Jewish immigrants, and brought up in lower-middle-class circumstances in London's south-west suburbs. 'Coming from that branch of East European Jewry that had embraced social democracy', he would explain, 'my own family was viscerally anti-Communist.'[3] Educated at a small South London private school, he served as national secretary of a Labour Zionist youth organization before going up to King's College, Cambridge in 1967. Post-graduate study took him to the Ecole Normale Supérieure in Paris, where he seems to have acquired his life-long distaste for Marxist intellectuals; and thence to southern France, where he undertook doctoral research on the history of French socialism in the Var. His first two books would draw extensively on this work: *La Reconstruction du Parti Socialiste, 1921–1926* was published in Paris in 1976; *Socialism in Provence, 1871–1914*, a 'study in the origins of the French left', appeared three years later.[4] The mid-70s was a time of heightened establishment concern in France at the prospect of a joint Socialist–PCF election victory, in the aftermath of the Portuguese revolution. This background informs the central preoccupation in both Judt's books with why France had failed to produce a reliable social-democratic party, on the Anglo-Nordic model. Unlike its solidly anti-Communist counterparts, the British Labour Party or German SDP, the Section Française de l'Internationale Ouvrière (SFIO) had never quite shed the lexicon of Marxism and still appealed to a notion of socialism even after 1945, when its political practice was otherwise quite 'acceptable'. The themes of his doctoral research would prove to be central to much of Judt's subsequent career.

I. THE FRENCH LEFT

Judt's first book, *The Reconstruction of the Socialist Party*, examined the re-establishment of the SFIO after its historic split at the 1920 Congress of Tours, where a large majority of the delegates had opted for the Third

---

[1] Respectively, Geoffrey Wheatcroft, *Guardian*, 9 August 2010; Timothy Garton Ash, NYRB, 20 August 2010; *Economist*, 12 August 2010; William Grimes, NYT, 7 August 2010.

[2] 'Fearless': *Economist*, 12 August 2010; 'prophetic': *Guardian*, 9 August 2010; 'formidable': Chris Patten, *Observer*, 11 April 2010; 'forceful lucidity': Fritz Stern, contribution to NYRB–CERI SciencesPo conference, 'Tony Judt: A Distinctive Presence Among Us', 23–25 June 2011; 'inoculated against revolutionary ideas': Samuel Moyn, contribution to NYRB–CERI SciencesPo conference.

[3] Judt, 'Elucubrations: The "Marxism" of Louis Althusser', *The New Republic*, 7 March 1994; collected in *Reappraisals: Reflections on the Forgotten Twentieth Century*, London 2008, p. 106.

[4] *La Reconstruction du Parti Socialiste, 1921–1926*, Paris 1976; future references will anglicize the title. *Socialism in Provence, 1871–1914: A Study in the Origins of the Modern French Left*, Cambridge 1979.

International and moved to found the Parti Communiste Française. In Judt's view, it was the presence of a militant PCF to its left that forced the SFIO leadership to compensate for its reformist political practice with verbal commitments to socialism. The SFIO rank and file insisted that the party 'remain what they had made it'; any attempts to dilute its message would have played into the hands of the PCF. As Judt put it:

> The way was narrow: a too marked *rapprochement* with the PCF could allow the more radical and rigid party to destroy it, but too sharp a break from the communists could lead to the loss of elements who had remained in the SFIO only on the condition that it retained a revolutionary Marxist position.[5]

The 1920 split had not cleanly separated reformists from revolutionaries, as happened in other northern European socialist parties after the Bolshevik Revolution; instead, a section of the left remained with the rump SFIO led by Léon Blum, constituting a majority of its membership. Apart from a small, right-wing faction, all the SFIO delegates rejected collaboration in bourgeois governments and advocated the dictatorship of the proletariat. Judt reported that Socialist mayors were obliged to get party approval before inaugurating Monuments to the Fallen, a sharply divisive issue for the party in the aftermath of the Great War. The SFIO leadership initially hung back from rejoining the reconstituted Second International, preferring to support the Union of Vienna, the '2.5 International' established by the Austro-Marxists, although it duly signed up in 1923. Rank-and-file attitudes exercised a decisive restraint on the SFIO's parliamentary leadership: in 1924 Blum and his fellow deputies were obliged to lend only external support to the Radical government under Edouard Herriot—as it pursued a programme of austerity at home, imperial war in Morocco and military occupation in the Ruhr—since the party membership would not tolerate full participation. Here was an example of the high price paid by the SFIO for the ideological 'rigidity' necessary for its survival, given the ever-present pressure from the left exercised by the PCF.[6]

The Reconstruction of the Socialist Party was rapturously received in liberal-Atlanticist circles in France, where it was published by the National Political Science Foundation with a fulsome preface by the ex-Communist

---

[5] *Reconstruction of the Socialist Party*, pp. 45; 154.
[6] *Reconstruction of the Socialist Party*, pp. 10; 62–3; 146; 195; 184.

Annie Kriegel, whom even Judt was later to describe as having gone from 'full-blooded party dogma to conservative anti-Communism'.[7] Its warnings of the baneful effect of the PCF had obvious lessons for those tempted by the Union of the Left in the mid-70s. Anti-Communism had been the standard ideology in the Anglophone world all through the Cold War; but in France it only really became a doxa in the mid-70s. Solzhenitsyn's *Gulag Archipelago* was translated in 1974 and François Furet's influential *Rethinking the French Revolution* was published in 1978. In this context, Judt's hostile account of the PCF's influence in the 1920s was the perfect calling card; a long-existent Anglo-American anti-Communism converged felicitously with a rising French one.

Judt's second book, *Socialism in Provence, 1871–1914*, tracked back to a time before the baneful influence of the Comintern had been felt, aiming to rescue a vision of the modern French left as 'neither a *victime du marxisme* nor the latest in a succession of crypto-Jacobins'.[8] Drawing again on his doctoral research in the Var, Judt argued that the areas of late-nineteenth-century Socialist success were districts where small peasant proprietors were predominant, rather than sharecroppers or day labourers. The collapse of agricultural prices in the last decades of the nineteenth century had radicalized this layer. Picking up on Eric Wolf's idea of the 'middle peasant', Judt suggested that their relative economic autonomy gave small proprietors the capacity for independent action, while their vulnerability to market conjunctures, especially after the turn to viniculture, made them supporters of state protection for agriculture. Early Socialist programmes spoke directly to smallholder interests; initially, the Var peasants were 'responding to an ideology which appealed to them in class terms' in lending the party their support. Subsequently, this attachment would congeal into an unbreakable political tradition: 'voting for the Socialists formed part of the "historical" character of Provençal life, long after the SFIO had ceased to perform any obvious function on behalf of the local population and had indeed lost much of its revolutionary character and programme.'[9] In sum, material interests explained the rise of socialism, culture its perdurance.

---

[7] Kriegel writes: 'A beautiful book, written with the concise vigour that only familiarity with the sources, implacable clarity of method, well-honed analytical thinking and the elegance of a highly strung discourse can supply': *Reconstruction of the Socialist Party*, p. i. For Judt's comment, see *Marxism and the French Left: Studies in Labour and Politics in France, 1830–1981*, Oxford 1986, p. 209.

[8] *Socialism in Provence*, p. ix.

[9] *Socialism in Provence*, pp. 236–7; see also pp. 229–30.

As a work of empirical scholarship *Socialism in Provence* towers over Judt's later output, its extensively documented analysis revealing a careful social historian. The last chapters turn towards a more general discussion of French politics and the peasantry. Judt's argument here is a familiar one: the persistence of a broadly Marxian socialism in France was due to the large number of peasant smallholders, combined with the early introduction of universal suffrage: both legacies of the French Revolution.[10] France's backwardness, far from being a disadvantage for socialism in France, explained why it had done so relatively well. Judt gave a nod to modernization theory, agreeing that 'the potential for revolution' is greatest 'in the early years of capitalist development'. But its explanation was limited in the French case, because socialism did not disappear as the country modernized.[11] Overall, however, the story was clear: French socialism rested above all on a peasant base, and as such was a consequence of economic backwardness.

In Furet's footsteps

In an unguarded moment, Judt himself would remark that 'at some point between 1973 and 1978 Marxism, and the study of its theoretical implications and resonances, lost its stranglehold upon the intellectual imagination in France, a grip it had exercised unbroken for a generation. In the space of less than a decade it became fashionable to be not just non-Marxist, but anti-Marxist.'[12] Indeed; both his early works chimed perfectly with the dominant Parisian mood. Judt's next book—he was ensconced, from 1980 to 1987, at St. Anne's College, Oxford as a PPE tutor—was also well-angled to catch this favourable wind. Published in 1986, *Marxism and the French Left* was Judt's first foray into intellectual history. It had an unusual structure, to say the least: dense chapters on the nineteenth-century labour movement and the fortunes of the SFIO from 1920–36 were followed by a highly polemical presentation of French Marxism during the *trente glorieuses* of 1945–75, topped off by a paean to Mitterrand's victory in 1981.

Linking these apparently disparate topics is a highly selective narrative of the French left, occluding the anti-Nazi Resistance—indeed, dispensing with any analysis of the PCF. An ostentatiously partisan tone and

---

[10] *Socialism in Provence*, p. 302.
[11] *Socialism in Provence*, p. 292.
[12] *Marxism and the French Left*, p. 170.

a marked decline in scholarship set *Marxism and the French Left* apart from Judt's earlier work; it also suffered from a notable deterioration in internal coherence, as Judt attempted to put forward two mutually contradictory arguments in the same breath. On the one hand *Marxism and the French Left* claimed, following Furet, that the French left had historically been blighted by an adherence to 'revolutionary doctrines', with little countervailing experience of Anglo-Saxon liberties. During the course of the nineteenth century, post-1789 republican traditions had segued into Marxian ones, facilitated by the overlap of the two between the 1860s and the 1930s. On the other hand, Judt informed his readers that it was only after 1945 that 'consistently critical attitudes to capitalism' had taken hold on the French left, though mercifully 'their hegemony has been brief; in the 1980s it is again no longer a requirement of the left that it condemn profit, economic exploitation and wealth', as Mitterrand's presidency had shown.[13]

The explanation that Judt had confidently offered for the persistence of the revolutionary tradition in his earlier works is—just as confidently— reversed, without a word of explanation, in *Marxism and the French Left*. In 1979 *Socialism in Provence* had depicted nineteenth-century France as an economically backward society, with a precociously developed state. In 1986 *Marxism and the French Left* presented it as an economically developed society with a backward, 'illiberal' state:

> France was an industrial society with all the characteristic industrial land-scaping—massive conurbations (Lille-Roubaix-Tourcoing, St Etienne), fast-growing metropolitan cities (Paris, of course, but also Marseilles, which grew from 185,000 to 315,000 during Louis Napoléon's reign), gross extremes of wealth and poverty.[14]

In promoting mid-nineteenth-century France to the rank of a fully industrialized society, Judt directly contradicted his previous account of the strength of French socialism being due to its anchorage in pre-industrial soil. Without ever mentioning this, he now offered a new explanation for the persistence of the revolutionary tradition: the repressiveness of the Second Empire. After the massacre of the workers in 1848, the French labour movement no longer saw the state as a neutral arbiter of class conflicts but rather as an instrument that 'would always be used at the expense of the working population'. The French, then, had never

---

[13] *Marxism and the French Left*, p. 10.
[14] *Marxism and the French Left*, p. 33.

experienced 'that political liberalization which so confounded observers and protagonists after 1848 in other countries.'[15]

The chapter on the inter-war experience of the SFIO in *Marxism and the French Left* similarly recasts, without explanation, Judt's earlier analysis in *Reconstruction of the Socialist Party*. Even after the split at the Congress of Tours, in which the PCF hived off most of the industrial working-class members, leaving the SFIO as a cross-class, regional party, Socialist leaders continued to stress extra-parliamentary agitation: 'for Blum, almost as much as for the party left, elections were a means to spread the socialist word, and only secondarily did they serve to elect men to parliament, or even a local council'. Whereas Judt earlier suggested that the reasons for the SFIO's failure to become a responsible social-democratic party lay in the existence of the PCF, he now argued that both the SFIO and the PCF were rooted in a common political culture, tainted by 'revolutionary doctrine'—much more in line with Furet's thinking.[16]

Marxism and the French Left's discussion of the post-war intellectual scene—Judt's first stab at Sartre—was strangely sandwiched between this chapter on the SFIO and another on Mitterrand. It asked why it was that French Marxism, backward in comparison to its German and Italian counterparts up until the 1930s, had flowered in the post-war period and then collapsed. According to Judt, this arc reflected the political strength of the PCF, whose attraction for the intelligentsia simply reflected the prestige of Stalin. 'As a theory of radical politics', he declared, 'Marxism died with Stalin'.[17] The argument fails the elementary test of chronology: the two greatest products of post-war French Marxism, Sartre's *Critique of Dialectical Reason* and Althusser's *Reading Capital*, were published in 1960 and 1968, respectively.[18] As intellectual history, this was crude and shoddy stuff, not least because of Judt's relentlessly polemical intent—Communism, Marxism and Stalinism predictably presented as interchangeable terms. Judt made no attempt to reconstruct the ideas of post-war French thinkers, instead flaunting the fact that he had been

---

[15] *Marxism and the French Left*, p. 96.
[16] *Marxism and the French Left*, pp. 149; 158–60.
[17] *Marxism and the French Left*, p. 236.
[18] More generally it could be argued that, like other forms of Western Marxism, French left-wing thought in this period developed in a context in which official communist parties seemed increasingly unable or unwilling to act; the main theoretical concepts of this tradition—reification, seriality, interpellation—were designed to explain the reproduction of capitalist social relations.

'selective' in his treatment and that his approach had been to deny them any 'intellectual autonomy'; why should anyone take Sartre, for example, 'very seriously'?[19] With protocols like this, it is not surprising that Judt's account was not only littered with Cold War grotesqueries—Sartre and Beauvoir making a 'daily contribution' to 'the enslavement of the satellite states'—but with extraordinary philological howlers: Althusser, radical critic of Hegel, transmogrified into a 'passionate Hegelian'; Régis Debray labelled a fellow-thinker of Lévy and Glucksmann as a theorist of 'totalitarianism', rather than famously contemptuous of both the *nouveaux philosophes* and their theories.[20]

Marxism and the French Left had, of course, a happy ending. Judt waxed lyrical about what he called Mitterrand's 'electoral revolution of 1981': after more than a century, French politics had finally been normalized. The new Parti Socialiste had broken out of its class, regional and religious ghettos; now a responsible reformist force, its only remaining task was to 'acquire the political culture of a party of government' like the Swedish or Austrian social democrats. Mitterrand's victory was 'a major turning point in French political history, of qualitatively greater significance than any hitherto'—'for the Socialists, 1981 was their finest hour'. Not only had Mitterrand and his party 'transformed national politics in France', but they had firmly dissociated the left from 'internationalism and anti-militarism' and could now be trusted on 'defence'.[21]

The French historian

Judt's first cycle of work, focused on France, comes to a close with *Marxism and the French Left*. How should it be assessed? Historiographically, the argument of *Socialism in Provence* is obviously superior to its successor. France's industrialization was relatively slow in the nineteenth century; it had a large artisan and peasant sector—still almost half the population in 1945; yet it had introduced effective male suffrage as early as 1848. But such an account, linking political consciousness to class structure, raised a problem for Judt: it was too Marxian. Indeed his discomfort with it was clear even in *Socialism in Provence* where, after carefully establishing the link between peasants' economic interests and the emergence

[19] *Marxism and the French Left*, p. 15.
[20] *Marxism and the French Left*, pp. 198; 229.
[21] *Marxism and the French Left*, pp. 296; 290; 295.

of socialism, he abruptly abandoned it, without theoretical or empirical motivation, to embrace a cultural explanation for the movement's continuing appeal. Whatever the risk of conceptual incoherence, the switch was effective as a sort of historiographical *cordon sanitaire*, insulating twentieth-century France from class analysis.

Even hedged and sterilized, however, *Socialism in Provence*'s attempt to link politics to class interests was beyond the pale in the mid-1980s, when Furet and his followers had entirely hegemonized the field. It was this, rather than any underlying intellectual problem, that surely explained Judt's tacitly revised interpretation in *Marxism and the French Left*, so dramatically at odds with his first. Yet the central premise on which this new version rested, that late-nineteenth century France was a politically backward society, is patently false. Judt attempted to assimilate the French, Italian, and Spanish states of the period into the same type,[22] but this did serious violence to their respective political histories. Universal male suffrage, for example, did not come to Italy until 1912, or Spain until 1931; it was definitively established in France by the 1880s. More importantly, France had created national representative institutions by the end of the eighteenth century, unlike any other large state on the European continent.

If Judt failed to provide a compelling historiographical explanation for the appeal of Marxism to a significant layer of French workers, peasants and intellectuals, what of his second argument: that its soft spot for *marxisant* precepts was responsible for the French left's lack of political success for most of the twentieth century? The issues here are complex, and Judt's thinking far from consistent. Clarity requires first defining what 'success' means. For Judt this was obvious enough: a 'normal' social democracy. But it is unclear from a strictly historical point of view why this should be the standard. Judt's doctoral thesis exemplifies the problem. One of the strengths of *Reconstruction of the Socialist Party* was its documentation of the broad ideological commitment to revolutionary socialism within the SFIO; Blum himself in the 1920s held that an 'impersonal dictatorship of the proletariat' was an absolute necessity. But in that case, the historical question is not: why did the SFIO fail to act as a reformist social-democratic party, but rather: why did the SFIO fail to live up to its own self-understanding and act

---

[22] *Marxism and the French Left*, p. 11.

as a revolutionary party? Judt had evidently registered this problem in his first book, admitting that, in the 1920s, a programme of revolutionary transformation 'did not lack plausibility'; but he characteristically dismissed this line of thinking, on the grounds that even to ask such questions would be to apply a 'logical' rather than a historical standard.[23] Historiographically, of course, the reverse is the case: Judt himself was applying an abstracted 'logical' standard, in judging the inter-war SFIO from the perspective of post-war social democracy.

The political dénouement of Judt's decade-long engagement with the history of the French left was his celebration of the Mitterrand era. But here too his analysis proved dud. According to his—albeit self-contradictory—arguments, the 'normalization' of French politics in the 1980s, with Mitterrand's victory and the elimination of the PCF as an electoral force, should have led at last to an effective social democracy. In fact, of course, Mitterrand's legacy was the introduction of a gallicized Thatcherite neo-liberalism and, after 1990, abandonment of the last vestiges of Gaullist foreign policy for full participation in the new Atlantic order. Yet if Judt's labours in the vineyard of French history produced decreasing historiographical or analytical rewards, his exposure to the methods of Furet and his disciples played a critical role in expanding his repertoire as a pro-Western polemicist. Handily, he would find in the 'ethical turn' fashionable in late Cold War Paris a rhetorical stance and sententious tone that married perfectly with anti-Communist sermonizing. So, in *Marxism and the French Left* he explained:

> To be a socialist today is to find oneself in one of two positions. On the one hand, you can be in favour of a generalized *moral project* which asserts itself in conscious defiance of capitalist (interest-related) priorities. Or else you must argue from a series of premises, stated or otherwise, which are still best characterized as 'marxism', and which entail firm commitment to certain propositions about the life span and self-destructive properties of capitalism.[24]

Judt went on to lament: 'it is the unwillingness of most socialists in France to think of themselves as engaged in a project of an essentially indeterminate and partial kind that prevents them adopting the first of the two approaches.' The second—any theory of capitalism as a system

---

[23] *Reconstruction of the Socialist Party*, pp. 88; 82; 91.
[24] *Marxism and the French Left*, p. 298; emphasis added.

with its own laws of motion—led, he asserted, straight to Soviet-style totalitarian Communism.[25]

2. MANHATTAN

In the late 1980s, apparently bored by French history (and by his wife),[26] Judt followed the trail blazed by Timothy Garton Ash and numerous others to Eastern Europe. Gorbachev's diplomacy had removed any obstacles to humanitarian tourism and the region was now thoroughly penetrated by missionaries from the EEC and IMF–World Bank. A crash course in Czech, and meetings with Michnik, Havel and Kis, equipped Judt to present his credentials to Washington in the form of a paper given at the Wilson Center in 1987, 'The Politics of Impotence?'. From the vantage point of 2009, Judt would explain Czechoslovakia as his Mitteleuropa destination of choice in terms of its edgier national-cultural stereotype: 'that distinctly Polish (or Russian) sense of cultural grandeur was precisely what I wanted to circumnavigate, preferring the distinctively Czech qualities of doubt, cultural insecurity, and sceptical self-mockery.'[27] At the time, however, his justification had been exactly the opposite: for Czechoslovakians, Judt suggested in 1987, 'the whole point of intellectual production is to bear moral witness'. Freed—as the interrogative ironization of the title tried to indicate—from any concrete political engagement by the force of circumstance, intellectuals like Havel answered to a higher 'moral responsibility', just as Judt had told French socialists to do. 'The Politics of Impotence?' reported that, since 1968, oppositional Marxism in Eastern Europe had been replaced by a healthy focus on 'rights'. Nevertheless, it warned, 'to the extent that socialism is associated with a variety of welfare provisions, social-security systems and guarantees, a "return" to capitalism would not be regarded with favour by most people.'[28]

Judt's re-location to the French Institute at New York University took place the same year, 1987. Shortly after, he scooped a $20 million bequest

---

[25] *Marxism and the French Left*, p. 298.
[26] Judt, *The Memory Chalet*, New York 2010, pp. 165–72.
[27] *Memory Chalet*, p. 171. Allowance should of course be made for the author's failing health after 2008.
[28] Judt, 'The Politics of Impotence?', in Judt et al., eds, *Debating the Nature of Dissent in Eastern Europe*, Washington 1987, pp. 38; 6–7; 13.

from the 80-year-old Manhattan socialite and former Ziegfeld Follies star Paulette Goddard, who had accumulated a fortune in the course of several marriages (Charlie Chaplin, Burgess 'The Penguin' Meredith, Erich Maria Remarque). NYU's Remarque Institute would open its doors in the late 90s, under Judt's direction.[29] In the meantime, he produced a further reworking of his thoughts on post-war French intellectuals: published in 1993, *Past Imperfect: French Intellectuals, 1944–1956* was coolly received by specialist scholars but garnered fawning reviews for the director of the Remarque Institute in the key power-and-prestige outlets of the American academy; it also won Judt his first commission from the *New York Review of Books*.[30]

To return once again to the subject of the post-war *rive gauche* might appear to have been flogging a dead horse, especially now that the Cold War had ended. But Judt seems to have felt that *Marxism and the French Left* had dealt with Sartre and his contemporaries too much in terms of French politics. Now—and with little further reading required—he would lambast their record in the larger global struggle of freedom against Communism, at greater length and brandishing loftier, if still ill-defined, concepts: justice, responsibility, morality and ethics. The Berlin Wall had fallen, but it still remained to extirpate any lingering trace of left-wing ideas. In France, a rabid anti-Sartrean literature had been accumulating since the late 1970s but little of it had yet appeared in English. Casting himself as a courageous moralist, Judt recycled its tropes—principally, that Sartre and Beauvoir were Stalinist apologists—rejecting any mere 'neutral historicist account': 'In seeking to explain something that is intrinsically unattractive, to which the reader would normally respond with distaste, one is not excused from the obligation to be accurate, but neither is one under a compelling obligation to pretend neutrality.'[31]

---

[29] As Judt would gloat in his final interview: 'When I explained at a lunch in St John's College, Cambridge how Remarque worked, how much cash we had and how free I was to spend it as I chose, you could see them gagging . . .': *Prospect*, July 2010.

[30] Judt, *Past Imperfect: French Intellectuals, 1944–1956*, Berkeley 1992. 'Anyone interested in the history of twentieth-century French intellectuals will race through the book *Past Imperfect* with unflagging attention': Robert Wohl, *Journal of Modern History*, 1995; 'undeniable power and importance': David Schalk, *American Historical Review*, 1994. For a better-informed critical account see Carlin Romano's review in *The Nation*, 26 April 1993.

[31] *Past Imperfect*, pp. 7–8.

Here, still more openly than in his previous work, Judt spurned any serious discussion of his subjects' thought: 'This book is neither a history of ideas nor a social history of French intellectuals'; it is about 'the marked absence of a concern with public ethics or political morality' in France—which Judt quickly interpreted, before the reader had time to murmur *Les mains sales*, as: 'why the French response to totalitarianism differed from that of intellectuals elsewhere'.[32] Although presented as an exercise in 'a peculiarly Anglo-Saxon tradition of intellectual history', the result had nothing to do with the Cambridge School; it was more like a posthumous contribution to the literature of the Congress for Cultural Freedom. Judt proceeded chiefly by undocumented assertion, anonymous attribution or conjunctive assimilation—typically: 'How, in the face of all this evidence, could intelligent people wilfully defend communism as the hope of the future and Stalin as the solution to the riddle of History?'—as though any thorough-going critic of capitalism was also necessarily a worshipper of Stalin.

Sartre's actual record on the Soviet Union—the criticisms of Stalinism in *What is Literature*, the excoriation of the camps and of the invasion of Hungary in *Les Temps modernes*—is simply scanted. 'Sartre's philosophical thought during the 30s and early 40s was quite devoid of political and social implications', writes Judt—the *War Diaries? Being and Nothingness?* 'Sartre's contemporary opinions precluded any attention to questions of ethics or morality'—*Saint Genet? Notebooks for an Ethics?* The French radical tradition was 'dominated by a combination of republican premises and Marxist projections, conflating the capacities of the state and the interests of the individual'—but wasn't Existentialism founded on the idea of radical individual freedom? 'One very special characteristic of the French style of thought has been the emphasis upon "totality", or the absolute'—unlike the Germans? There is a Gallic 'distaste for intellectual doubt, uncertainty or scepticism'—Descartes?[33]

Past Imperfect's main argument, tirelessly reiterated, was that French left-wing intellectuals in this period lacked 'any common ideal of justice'—although Judt also remarked at one point that there was no 'consensus about justice' in France as a whole, either; and indeed offered no conceptualization of his own.[34] The result of this moral vacuum, he concluded, was to undermine French liberalism itself:

---

[32] *Past Imperfect*, p. 10.
[33] *Past Imperfect*, pp. 3; 80–1; 241; *Marxism and the French Left*, p. 174.
[34] *Past Imperfect*, pp. 74; 145–6.

What was missing, then, in the political language of contemporary France were the central premises, the building blocks of a liberal political vision . . . Quite absent was the liberal assumption of a necessary and desirable space between the individual and the collective, the private and the public, society and the state.[35]

By any measure Tocqueville, Constant and Guizot would appear rather substantial French liberal 'building blocks', constituting a richer tradition than that of nineteenth-century Britain, which produced little more than Mill. But it was the absence of a liberal 'political vision', not a theoretical tradition, that Judt was lamenting. Like the French left, liberalism in the Hexagon had also unfortunately 'historicized' the moral idea of rights, by relating them to 1789. In sum, French liberals failed to grasp that liberalism is 'not about some sort of liberal project for society: it is about a society in which the messiness and openness of politics precludes the application of large-scale projects, however rational and ideal.'[36] The 'generalized moral project' that Judt had extolled seven years before, in Marxism and the French Left—'a project of an essentially indeterminate and partial kind'—was unceremoniously abandoned in Past Imperfect. Projects were now out; only the moral 'vision' was now of value.[37] (Indeed Judt appeared at this stage to have abandoned social democracy as well, preferring to speak of a more inclusive 'liberalism'.)

The intellectual configuration in France in the early 1990s was, of course, the very opposite of Judt's representation of it. The liberalism of Furet and company was unquestionably the hegemonic ideology of the period. In a ludicrous inversion, Judt depicted it as the lonely, marginal thinking of a tiny minority, allowing him to offer his own thoroughly conventional book as a—tacitly, brave—contribution to heterodoxy, along with theirs.[38] But politically, Past Imperfect suggested that, just as, even after Mitterrand, French social democracy could never quite come up to British or Nordic standards, so French liberals were 'unable to commit themselves to the utilitarian or ethical individualism of their British contemporaries' in the nineteenth century, and even today 'few thinkers in France have so far undertaken to construct a moral vocabulary for liberal

[35] Past Imperfect, p. 241.
[36] Past Imperfect, pp. 235–9; 240; 315.
[37] Marxism and the French Left, p. 298; Past Imperfect, p. 315.
[38] Past Imperfect, p. 315, fn 33.

politics, an ethics, so to speak, of democracy.'[39] Even with the PCF banished to the fringes, France remained insufficiently Anglo-Saxon.

Pantheon

Judt's next book returned to the subject of French intellectuals, this time focused not on his villains, but on his heroes. *The Burden of Responsibility: Blum, Camus, Aron and the French Twentieth Century* appeared in 1998, dedicated, appropriately enough, to the memory of François Furet. Once again, Judt paid little attention to his subjects' ideas: according to *Burden of Responsibility*, Blum made no contribution to socialist theory, Camus was unpolitical, Aron overvalued philosophy.[40] Judt explained that this was a study of political 'responsibility', in contrast to the analysis of political 'irresponsibility' in his previous book. His three exemplars, Blum, Camus and Aron, stood out against the three 'intersecting forms of irresponsibility'—political, moral and intellectual—that 'shaped French public life from the end of the First World War until the middle of the 1970s'. Indeed the irresponsibility of French intellectuals had expanded considerably since *Past Imperfect*, when they had at least, according to Judt, seen themselves as responsible to history, if not to other people.[41] But what did the two contrasting terms actually mean? *The Burden of Responsibility* provides a distinctly unhelpful tautology, defining 'irresponsibility' as 'the propensity in various spheres of public life to neglect or abandon intellectual, moral or political responsibility'. Judt clarifies: 'In addition to the qualities of courage and integrity, Blum, Aron, and Camus have something else in common. They were all anti-Communists.'[42] As the *New York Times* reviewer of *Past Imperfect* had laconically remarked, Judt's idea of a responsible intellectual was simply one whose views he found sympathetic.[43]

---

[39] *Past Imperfect*, pp. 240; 316.
[40] Judt, *The Burden of Responsibility: Blum, Camus, Aron and the French Twentieth Century*, Chicago 1998, pp. 53; 104; 170–2.
[41] *Past Imperfect*, pp. 22; 121.
[42] *Burden of Responsibility*, pp. 20; 22.
[43] NYT, 10 January 1993; see John Sturrock, *The Word from Paris*, London 1998, p. 12. In addition to their anti-Communism, Blum and Aron were commended for their Zionism and Anglophilia. Blum's betrayal of the Spanish Republic was waved away, since 'he was truly constrained' by Britain, of whose system of government he was a 'fervent admirer'. Aron's occasional weakness for Gallic philosophical pretensions was redeemed by his commitment to the 'English or Anglo-American school of thought' about politics: *Burden of Responsibility*, pp. 47; 145–7.

If Judt had no difficulty establishing the 'absolute clarity on the Communist question' of his trio, he systematically downplayed their complicity with imperialism.[44] Yet Blum's first act, as a *chef de cabinet* in the 1914 *Union Sacrée* government, was to betray the Socialists' solemn pre-war promise not to participate in the mutual slaughter of the Great War. In 1925, at the height of the Rif colonial war, he informed the Assembly that there was 'not only a right, but a duty for what are known as the superior races to draw towards themselves the races which have not attained the same degree of culture and civilisation'. Becoming Prime Minister again in December 1945, four weeks after the bombardment of Haiphong that launched the French war in Indochina, he explained that the colonial mission of France was 'not yet accomplished'. Camus, who said virtually nothing about the war in Indochina, was dismissed even by Aron as no more than 'a well-intentioned colonizer' in Algeria.[45] Both Camus and Aron approved the Anglo-French-Israeli aggression against Egypt in 1956, Aron warning of the 'Führer on the Nile' and Camus of the menace of Soviet-backed 'Arab imperialism'. Aron himself backed both the French and the American wars in Indochina, and objected to the French war in Algeria not on ethical grounds but because the French civilizing mission, however laudable in itself, 'would be unsustainably expensive'.[46] When asked why he never spoke out against French torture in Algeria, Aron replied that he had never known anyone speak in favour of torture, so what was the point? Judt appears to be perfectly satisfied with this example of moral responsibility, whose logic is that the subject need never have been mentioned.

An allusion to Weber's classic discussion of the ethics of responsibility illustrated Judt's tenuous grasp of the complex issues raised by this highly charged term. The 'Weberian calculus', as he glossed it, entailed 'the sense that we can behave responsibly without making partisan commitments—or else that a partisan engagement may under

---

[44] Opposition to the Algerian War had already been reduced to little more than an 'adventure' for the intelligentsia in *Past Imperfect*, where anti-colonialism was accused of simplifying a complex matter, presenting it as a 'straightforward moral choice': *Past Imperfect*, pp. 287; 283. But this is precisely what Judt demanded with regard to state socialism.

[45] *Burden of Responsibility*, p. 95.

[46] *Burden of Responsibility*, p. 166. Judt had calmly written elsewhere of Camus's 'rejection of violence': 'Albert Camus: "The best man in France"', NYRB, 6 October 1994.

certain circumstances be the responsible option'.[47] Weber's actual view was rather different. For the great sociologist, the ethic of responsibility was embodied by the political actor who took responsibility for the use of 'legitimate violence'. He warned, in 'Politics as a Vocation', that 'Whomsoever contracts with violent means—and every politician does— is exposed to its specific consequences.' Ultimately, the political figure faced a choice between one way of using violence and another, without an adequate standard for discriminating between them; to act politically, then, required an absolute belief in the rightness of one's own cause, in order to transcend the chasm between political ends and means. An ethic of conviction and an ethic of responsibility were not 'absolute contrasts, but rather supplements'.[48] Indeed, Weber's concept of political responsibility here was not far from Sartre's view, a fact that Judt naturally does not confront. As Sartre put the point, in his long essay in *Les Temps modernes* following the Hungarian revolution:

> In the worst case, the assumption of a moral position disguises the operation of a politician; in the best it does not affect the facts and the moralist misses the point. But politics, of whatever sort, is an action undertaken in common with certain men against other men.[49]

Both Sartre and Weber refused the comfortable stance of the moralizer because they were aware of the tension between ethics and politics, and did not try to obscure it with high-sounding bromides.

3. EUROPE

By the mid-90s the *New York Review of Books* was offering Judt a more prominent platform, as publicist and commentator, than scholarly work could provide. After his first appearance there in August 1993, reviewing a work on the fate of French Jews under the Vichy regime, Judt became a regular fixture, contributing three or four pieces a year over the next decade. Eventually he would rival, or even overtake, Garton Ash and Buruma in his frequency as a quasi-editorialist, pronouncing not just on France but on Eastern Europe, the lessons of the Cold War and the fate of the West in general. The year 1993 also saw his

---

[47] *Burden of Responsibility*, p. 145.
[48] From *Max Weber: Essays in Sociology*, Hans Gerth, ed., Oxford 1958.
[49] Jean-Paul Sartre, *Situations VII*, Paris, 1965, p. 147.

first contribution to *The New Republic*: an attack on Althusser, 'the Paris strangler'. He would soon join the magazine's editorial board.[50] The posture Judt had developed in the course of his assaults on the French left—tailing-ending the liberal-establishment vanguard, while portraying himself as a courageous exception, a lone moral voice— served him well within this wider field. In 1995–96, as Clinton and Albright elbowed aside Kohl and Mitterrand to knock ex-Yugoslav heads together, Judt lamented the failure of European leadership. In 1997, as the prophets of the Third Way took up residence in Downing Street, he called for a new social-liberal agenda. He lauded Blair's 'firm and honourable stand' on Kosovo and endorsed the Oslo Accords on Palestine.[51] In *The New Republic* he contributed to a 1997 'Zionism at 100' symposium—arguing that Zionism should not be seen as an ethno-nationalist movement, but a universalist-enlightenment one— and attacked Peter Novick's critique of the instrumentalization of the Judeocide in *The Holocaust in American Life*.[52]

In 2008 Judt would publish a selection of these writings in *Reappraisals*, appointing himself as a memorializer to the contemporary world on the lessons of 'the forgotten twentieth century'; such overlooked themes as vigilance against Communism and Holocaust recognition taking pride of place. In his Introduction, Judt regretted that the term 'intellectual' had come to evoke a 'narrow band of left-leaning "progressives"', with Sartre at their head, rather than his own pantheon: Camus, Koestler and Kołakowski. Judt's paean to the last, in keeping with his general approach to the history of ideas, managed to avoid any mention of Kołakowski's religious conversion, inconvenient for Judt as a sharp critic of Woytila.[53]

Unsurprisingly, perhaps, Judt's historical research took a back seat during this period. His only book between 1993 and 2005 was a slender

---

[50] Anti-Communism continued to be a salient theme: 'it was the palpably malign quality of the Great Socialist Experiment', Judt opined, that 'made it so irresistible to men and women of goodwill in search of a Cause'. Judt, 'The Information', TNR, 4 November 2002.

[51] Judt, 'Europe: The Grand Illusion', NYRB, 11 July 1996; 'The Social Question Redivivus', *Foreign Affairs*, Sept–Oct 1997; 'The Gnome in the Garden', NYRB, 19 July 2001.

[52] Judt, 'Zionism at 100', TNR, 8 September 1997; 'The Morbid Truth', TNR, 19 July 1999.

[53] Judt, *Reappraisals*, p. 129.

volume containing three lectures, two of them already published in the NYRB, which appeared as *A Grand Illusion? An Essay on Europe* in 1996. No rationale was provided for the switch from French socialism to the larger, more nebulous subject of 'Europe' as a historical subject. In his NYRB obituary, Timothy Snyder—demonstrating an astonishing ignorance of his colleague's actual trajectory—would suggest that it was Judt's 'midlife participation in Eastern European intellectual life, which hastened the break with Marxism [*sic*] and enabled a more capacious view of the continent.'[54] But although he liked to term himself an 'Eastern Europeanist', Judt never produced any monograph on the region; even his 1987 'A Politics of Impotence?' remained a working paper.

The political tone of *A Grand Illusion?* was distinctly Euro-pessimist: 'a truly united Europe is sufficiently unlikely for it to be unwise and self-defeating to insist on it'. The exceptionally favourable combination of circumstances that drove European integration forward up to the 1980s would not reappear:

> These were unrepeatable, one-time transformations. That is to say, Western Europe will probably never again have to catch up on thirty years of economic stagnation or half a century of agrarian depression, or rebuild after a disastrous war. Nor will it be bound together by the need to do so, or by the coincidence of Communist threat and American encouragement.[55]

Extension to the East could not occur on the terms granted to existing member states, since this would require huge transfer payments from Western European economies already suffering from persistent unemployment and slow growth. Long-running economic divergences between the two halves of Europe, dating back to before 1914, constituted a major obstacle to unification. Moreover, the lessons of Yugoslavia—this was written at the moment of the Dayton Accords—illustrated 'the weakness of European initiatives, the compulsion to avoid engagement and the absence of any recognized collective strategic interest beyond maintaining the status quo'. 'In its strong form', Judt concluded, 'the idea of Europe has had its day.'[56]

---

[54] Timothy Snyder, 'On Tony Judt', NYRB, 14 October 2010. Snyder is co-author with Judt of a 'history of the life of the mind in the twentieth century', due out later this year.

[55] Judt, *A Grand Illusion? An Essay on Europe*, New York 1996, pp. viii; 33.

[56] *Grand Illusion?*, pp. 92–7; 60; 137; 128.

Cause célèbre

At the turn of the century, commentary in the NYRB and *New Republic* continued to claim much of Judt's time. His response to 9.11 announced that the world had crossed the threshold into a new moral-political universe. He rallied immediately behind the war in Afghanistan and organized an October 2002 conference on the central war-on-terror theme of 'global anti-Americanism'. Like millions of others, however, he was dubious about Bush and Cheney's plans for the invasion of Iraq; also about the salience of the settlers' agenda in Israeli politics. In July 2002 he wrote a piece mildly critical of 'intolerant, ultra-religious' settlers and anti-Arab *mizrahi* Israelis in *The New Republic*. The following year his NYRB article, 'Israel: The Alternative', created a furore in New York. As Judt would recall, 'the rabbis of Riverside' picketed a talk he was due to give at a local high school, marshalling protesters dressed as concentration-camp inmates.[57] The event says more about the thuggishness of hardline American Zionists than it does about Judt's essay, which recycled the venerable notion of a bi-national democracy for Israel–Palestine.

The Oslo process was now over, Judt declared: 'Israel continues to mock its American patron, building illegal settlements in general disregard of the "road map".' The US president had been 'reduced to a ventriloquist's dummy, pitifully reciting the Israeli cabinet's line: "It's all Arafat's fault".' Palestinian Arabs, 'corralled into bantustans', subsisted on EU handouts. Sharon, Arafat and a handful of terrorists could all 'claim victory'. Departing from his previous assertion that Zionism had been a universalist movement, he declared it a typical late-nineteenth-century ethno-nationalist one, and as such an anachronism in 'a world that has moved on, a world of individual rights, open frontiers and international law'. Given the demographic trend towards a Palestinian majority in 'greater Israel', the country would now have to choose between being a non-democratic ethno-religious state, with a growing majority of disenfranchised non-Jews, or a multi-cultural, multi-ethnic secular democracy. Israel was already 'a multi-cultural society in all but name', yet ranked its citizens according to ethno-religious criteria. Furthermore, 'Israel's behaviour has been a disaster for American foreign policy'— 'Washington's unconditional support for Israel even in spite of (silent)

---

[57] *Prospect*, August 2010.

misgivings is the main reason why most of the world no longer credits our good faith':

> It is now tacitly conceded by those in a position to know that America's reasons for going to war in Iraq were not necessarily those advertised at the time. For many in the current US Administration, a major consideration was the need to destabilize and then reconfigure the Middle East in a manner thought favourable to Israel.[58]

Formerly, the existence of the state of Israel had allowed Jews to 'walk tall'. Now, however—the actual tipping-point is not specified—its behaviour left non-Israeli Jews 'exposed to criticism and vulnerable to attack for things they didn't do'—'the depressing truth is that Israel today is bad for the Jews'. The situation had corroded American domestic debate: 'Rather than think straight about the Middle East, American politicians and pundits slander our European allies when they dissent, speak glibly and irresponsibly of resurgent anti-Semitism when Israel is criticized and censoriously rebuke any public figure at home who tries to break from the consensus'—Judt apparently forgetting his own censorious rebuke of Novick a few years before. The *volte face* on Israel led to Judt's ejection from *The New Republic*'s editorial board and a rabid riposte from his former friend Leon Wieseltier, its literary editor, who pointed out accurately enough that the idea of a one-state solution, far from requiring anyone to 'think the unthinkable', as Judt had written, was a notion as old as the conflict over Palestine itself.[59]

Judt did not include the Israel essay in his 2008 collection *Reappraisals* and seems scarcely to have addressed the one-state solution again. But reckless neo-conservative interventionism and the crudity of right-wing American Zionism had clearly soured him on the society of which he was now a citizen. In early 2005 the NYRB published Judt's 'The Good Society: Europe vs America', which strongly favoured the former. A few months later *Postwar*, his 900-page history of Europe since 1945, appeared. The idea of writing on the 1945–89 period had apparently come to Judt in December 1989, within a month of the fall of the Berlin Wall: 'the history of post-war Europe would need to be rewritten'—in retrospect, the epoch would seem 'a post-war parenthesis, the unfinished business of a conflict that ended in 1945 but whose epilogue had lasted for another half

---

[58] Judt, 'Israel: The Alternative', NYRB, 23 October 2003.
[59] Wieseltier, 'Israel, Palestine and the Return of the Bi-National Fantasy', TNR, 27 October 2003.

century'.[60] In the event, *Past Imperfect, A Grand Illusion?* and book reviewing had intervened. By the time the book came to be written, Judt's view of Europe had undergone a dramatic revision.

Exemplary Europe

For the most part, *Postwar* offered a familiar narrative of the period, somewhat meandering in structure and largely focused on the West; coverage of Eastern Europe mostly functioned as a sombre counterpoint to the main melody. Opening with a survey of the state of Europe after World War Two, the book covered the onset of Cold War, the advent of western affluence and the 'social democratic moment'; the 1960s, East and West; accelerated EEC integration, as a response to 1970s economic turbulence; the new Hayekian 'realism' of the 1980s, in both Thatcherite and *mitterrandiste* forms; Solidarność, Gorbachev and the fall of the Comecon regimes in 1989; German reunification, Maastricht, the break-up of Yugoslavia and EU expansion. Into this lengthy, often rather flat account, Judt inserted what he confessed was 'an avowedly personal interpretation'. Post-war Europe, he argued, had produced not just the integrated structures of the EU but a social model that stood as a moral 'beacon' to aspirant members and a 'global challenge' to the American way of life. Europe had emerged, at the dawn of the twenty-first century, as a 'paragon of the international virtues':

> a community of values and a system of inter-state relations held up by Europeans and non-Europeans alike as an exemplar for all to emulate. In part this was the backwash of growing disillusion with the American alternative; but the reputation was well earned . . . Neither America nor China had a serviceable model to propose for universal emulation. In spite of the horrors of their recent past—and in large measure because of them—it was *Europeans* who were now uniquely placed to offer the world some modest advice on how to avoid repeating their own mistakes. Few would have predicted it sixty years before, but the twenty-first century might yet belong to Europe.[61]

Judt's argument might be read as a grand narrative for today's Eurocracy, analogous to the uplifting national tales of the early twentieth century, such as Volpe's *Italia in Cammino* or Marshall's *Our Island Story*. His aim seems to have been to produce a synthesis of his now-revived admiration

---

[60] Judt, *Postwar: A History of Europe Since 1945*, New York 2005, p. 2.
[61] *Postwar*, pp. xiii; 7–8; 799–800.

for social democracy and his hopes for the EU as an alternative to Bush's America. The 'European social model' became the new pole of attraction for Judt's politics: more acceptable than the neo-conservative US and less *passé* than the labour movement itself. But the attempt to conflate European integration, the post-war welfare state and the record of the social-democratic parties into an exemplar for the twenty-first century ended in analytical incoherence. *Postwar* oscillated continually between the assertion that 'welfare capitalism' was non-partisan, 'truly post-ideological', and the claim that it was a quintessentially social-democratic creation. On the one hand, the welfare state was the result of a 'deep longing for normality' produced by the inter-war age of extremes and the lessons of World War Two. For the generation of 1945, 'some workable balance between political freedoms and the rational, equitable distributive function of the administrative state seemed the only sensible route out of the abyss'. This meant 'a broad consensus not to press inherited ideological or cultural divisions to the point of political polarization' and a 'de-politicized citizenry', capped by 'reform-minded' Christian Democrat parties and 'a parliamentary Left'. On the other hand, welfare capitalism was the 'distinctive vision' of social democracy, which held that 'genuine improvements in the condition of all classes could be obtained in incremental and peaceful ways'.[62]

Judt drives home the importance of a social-democratic party to final outcomes by contrasting Scandinavia and Eastern Europe. The reason that Sweden, in particular, did not develop in the same way as 'other economically depressed societies on the European margin between the wars' was due to the Social Democrats. By renouncing 'radical dogma and revolutionary ambitions', the Swedish SAD was able to incorporate small-holding peasants and strike a deal with Swedish capital at Saltsjöbaden in 1938. More generally:

> The embittered and destitute peasants of inter-war central and southern Europe formed a ready constituency for Nazis, Fascists or single-issue Agrarian populists. But the equally troubled farmers, loggers, crofters and fishermen of Europe's far north turned in growing numbers to the Social Democrats, who actively supported agrarian cooperatives . . . and thereby blurred the longstanding socialist distinctions between private production and collectivist goals, 'backward' country and 'modern' town that were so electorally disastrous in other countries.[63]

---

[62] *Postwar*, pp. 362; 83; 77; 263; 363.
[63] *Postwar*, pp. 364–5.

The notion of a peasant-based social democracy as the road not taken in inter-war Eastern Europe is, of course, completely unhistorical. Agriculture there was profoundly backward at the time; when popular uprisings weakened landed elites, as happened in Romania, the underlying organization of production tended to revert back to subsistence farming. The agrarian economy simply did not produce adequate surpluses for a sustained modernization drive. This was one reason for the similarity among the modernizing political movements there: liberal, fascist or Communist, all faced the basic problem of extracting sufficient surplus from the peasant sector to industrialize. The choice in Eastern Europe was never really between social democracy and Leninism, but among structurally similar modernizing regimes with different ideological labels. The situation in Scandinavia, particularly in Sweden, was entirely different: a substantial free-holder peasantry existed there, literacy was widespread and agrarian surpluses were much higher. Peasants were never 'equally troubled' in Scandinavia. In general, regional social democracy operated in such a uniquely favourable environment that it was never available as a model for export, as most of its leaders recognized.

Judt's argument in *Postwar* further oscillated between claims that the welfare state has been in serious danger since the 1970s and declarations that it was the cornerstone of the twenty-first-century European social model. The first argument, based on a decidedly sketchy political economy—not a strong suit for Judt, as *Postwar* showed—claimed that, by the early 1970s, the profit margins that had made the social-democratic class compromise possible came under threat, as the 'migration of surplus agricultural labour into productive urban industry' had ended and 'rates of productivity increase began inexorably to decline'; Keynesian stimulus policies created inflation while failing to generate growth. Furthermore, the 'white, male, employed working class', whose social-democratic parties had spearheaded the welfare state, was starting to contract. On the other hand, Judt claimed that it had survived robustly through all the ideological and political din about it. 'Economic liberalization did not signal the fall of the welfare state, nor even its terminal decline, notwithstanding the hopes of its theorists. It did, though, illustrate'—strange choice of verb—'a seismic shift in the allocation of resources and initiative from public to private sectors.'[64]

---

[64] *Postwar*, pp. 456; 484; 558.

Postwar's paean to the European social model stood in striking contrast to the gloomy outlook of *A Grand Illusion?*, which received no mention. The two books also offered sharply different accounts of Europe's east-west divide. In 1995, Judt had disputed the notion that the division was 'an artificial creation of the Cold War, an iron curtain gratuitously and recently drawn across a single cultural space.' On the contrary, as early as the fifteenth century there had been 'an invisible line that already ran from north to south through the middle of Europe.' To extend EU membership to the ex-Communist European countries would be 'an act of charity'.[65] Without a word of explanation, *Postwar* reverses these claims: the division is entirely a creation of the Cold War; before World War Two, 'the differences between North and South, rich and poor, urban and rural, counted for more than those between East and West.' After 1945, however:

> The effect of the Sovietization of Eastern Europe was to draw it steadily away from the western half of the continent. Just as Western Europe was about to enter an era of dramatic transformation and unprecedented prosperity, Eastern Europe was slipping into a coma: a winter of inertia and resignation, punctured by cycles of protest and subjugation, that would last for nearly four decades.[66]

In this reading, the advance of the Soviet *glacis* had blocked the region's chance of establishing an indigenous welfare state. Judt's contrary argument in 'Politics of Impotence?'—that central Europeans were so attached to their states' welfare provisions that they might not look kindly on the restoration of capitalism—had evidently been forgotten.

Judt's encomium to the European social model is further undermined by the second, less tendentious strand of his narrative: a rather humdrum account of European integration. As a historian, Judt had little talent for bringing protagonists to life—indeed, little interest in character as such—and *Postwar* offered no fresh interpretation or archival discoveries. Yet the bare facts it presented on the transnational agreements that eventually produced the EU showed that, whatever one might say about the European social model, it was a historical theme quite independent from that of European union. None of the key stages on the path to integration had much to do with the welfare state; they were mostly the

---

[65] *Grand Illusion?* pp. 46–7; 130.
[66] *Postwar*, p. 195.

result of geo-political calculations and, from the late 1980s, basically neo-liberal. The 1950 Schuman Plan had allowed Germany to escape from Allied economic controls, while providing a guarantee to the French against German re-armament. As Judt himself pointed out, the European Economic Community was an attempt to open French and German markets, again for largely political reasons. The impetus towards establishing a European monetary system came from an attempt to stabilize exchange rates, after the collapse of the Bretton Woods system. The creation of the European Union, through the 1987 Single European Act and 1992 Maastricht Treaty, established the free circulation of goods, services and capital among its members but also imposed harsh German-style budgetary requirements. As *Postwar* noted, Eurozone finance ministers would be 'unable to respond to the Siren-calls of voters and politicians for easier money and increased public spending'.[67]

Judt attempted to resolve this tension between the actual dynamics of European integration and his supposed European social model through some implausible rhetorical linkages—for example:

> In relative terms, the so-called 'social' element in the EU budget was tiny—less than 1 percent of GNP. But from the late Eighties, the budgets of the European Community and the Union nevertheless had a distinctively redistributive quality, transferring resources from wealthy regions to poor ones and contributing to a steady reduction in the aggregate gap between rich and poor: substituting in effect, for the nationally based Social-Democratic programmes of an earlier generation.[68]

This was to confuse wish with reality. Judt himself pointed out twenty pages later that regional and social inequalities in Europe had sharply increased since the 1980s: a small super-rich core now contrasted with the poorer regions of the Mediterranean zone and Eastern Europe. Rather than scaling up a welfarist model, European integration had if anything undermined it.

What of the 'social model' itself? Judt suggested that, in sharp contrast to the United States, European societies were marked by high taxes, long vacations, free healthcare, good public education and high life expectancy. But the relation between this ideal and actually existing European societies remained unclear. Mostly Judt seemed to be imagining a loose

---

[67] *Postwar*, pp. 305, 461, 715.
[68] *Postwar*, pp. 732.

conceptual average of Europe's rich northwest—Belgium, Denmark, Britain, Ireland, France, Germany, Norway—rather than the uneven social topography of the continent as a whole. Although they were discussed in passing in *Postwar*, the unequal societies of Europe's south and east—Portugal, Spain, Italy, Greece—were never allowed to impinge on its 'social model'.[69] Nor, finally, does Judt's attempt to counter-pose a 'good' European model to a 'bad' American one stand up. As his own narrative made clear, post-war Europe was closely shaped by US interventionism; Washington took extraordinary measures to reconstruct Western Europe's economies and to provide its states with a security guarantee that removed the need to rearm. Historically, the 'European model', however specified, has never been an alternative to American hegemony, but rather a consequence of it.

4. SOCIAL DEMOCRACY?

The fragility of Judt's attempted synthesis in *Postwar* was most evident in its rapid breakdown. By the time of his last book, *Ill Fares the Land*, he had undergone another conversion in political outlook. The book originated as a valedictory lecture at NYU in 2009, given after Judt had been diagnosed with amyotrophic lateral sclerosis. A transcription of the lecture had been published in the NYRB, bringing a 'chorus of demands for its expansion into a little book'. The resulting political testament struck a declamatory note: 'Something is profoundly wrong with the way we live today'—'and yet we seem unable to conceive of alternatives'.[70] *Ill Fares the Land* sought to provide one, in the form of a rehabilitated social democracy. Alas for his admirers, the results contradicted or flatly reversed many of Judt's most confident pronouncements on the welfare state and social democracy in *Postwar*. The resulting confusion was amply demonstrated in his attempts to grapple with four key questions.

(i) The welfare state—who created it?

Judt wanted to maintain once again that the welfare state was both the product of a cross-party 'Keynesian consensus' and a historic social-democratic achievement. But whereas *Postwar* had celebrated the

---

[69] *Postwar*, pp. 792; 777–800.
[70] *Ill Fares the Land*, New York 2010, pp. xiv, 1–2.

superiority of Europe's social model, *Ill Fares the Land* played down any such contrast, arguing instead that Roosevelt's New Deal and Johnson's Great Society were in practice the American version of social democracy.[71] The 'longing for normality' after World War Two that had explained Europeans' special predilection for state-administered welfare in *Postwar* now apparently applied to Americans as well. A continual slippage in Judt's use of the term 'social democracy' sometimes allowed it to suggest a form of Hegelian historical reason, an 'objective' purpose that escapes the 'subjective' intentions of those involved. Thus anyone who supported post-war Keynesian demand management gets promoted to the rank of 'objective' social democrat—and larded with praise—whatever his or her party label:

> Not only did social democrats sustain full employment for nearly three decades, they also maintained growth rates more than competitive with those of the untrammelled market economies of the past. And on the back of these economic successes they introduced radically disjunctive social changes that came to seem, within a short span of years, quite normal. When Lyndon Johnson spoke of building a 'great society' on the basis of massive public expenditure on a variety of government-sponsored programs and agencies, few objected and fewer still thought the proposition odd.[72]

Supporters of Eugene McCarthy—indeed, LBJ himself—might be surprised at this retrospective elevation to the status of a Yankee Olof Palme.

Similarly, while *Postwar* had given pride of place to Scandinavian and British social democracy, *Ill Fares the Land* explained that 'pure' social democracy along Scandinavian lines had always been 'non-exportable', while the welfare state created by post-war British Labour was not really social democratic at all, but simply 'pragmatic'. Accompanying this was a much more pronounced emphasis on the non-radicalism of the welfare state, now not just 'post-ideological', as in *Postwar*, but the creation of 'instinctive conservatives'.[73] By Judt's criteria, indeed, Berlusconi, Sarkozy and Merkel might count as social democrats:

> Social democracy, in one form or another, is the prose of contemporary European politics. There are very few European politicians, and fewer still in positions of influence, who would dissent from core social democratic assumptions about the duties of the state, however much they might differ as to their scope.[74]

---

[71] *Ill Fares the Land*, p. 32.
[73] *Ill Fares the Land*, pp. 69; 51; 46.

[72] *Ill Fares the Land*, p. 79.
[74] *Ill Fares the Land*, p. 143.

The conceptual muddiness of this approach, in which virtually all political actors become the unwitting instruments of a social-democratic *Geist*, succeeds only in obscuring the central political and historical issues: what was the actual role of social-democratic parties in the construction of the welfare state, and what part was played by broader political-economic conditions? These were questions that Judt never even posed. Two essential components to any answer might be stressed, though: firstly, the long economic boom of the post-war period, which has little if any linkage to the strength of social-democratic parties but whose arc tracks the expansion of welfarism very closely. Secondly, the existence of a rival Communist bloc, proclaiming itself the homeland of the workers. The conversion of social-democratic parties into neo-liberal centre lefts followed the decline and fall of the state-socialist challenge. Judt, the life-long anti-Communist, at one point lets this slip himself:

> That is why the fall of Communism mattered so much. With its collapse, there unravelled the whole skein of doctrines that had bound the Left together for over a century. However perverted the Muscovite variation, its sudden and complete disappearance could not but have a disruptive impact on any party or movement calling itself 'social democratic' . . . for the Left, the absence of a historically buttressed narrative leaves an empty space.[75]

However one defines the relationship, empirically it seems clear that social democracy has been deeply dependent on its revolutionary twin. The attempt to formulate a social-democratic politics in the absence of a socialist one would seem historically implausible.

(ii) The welfare state—what went wrong?

Without explanation, the boosterism of *Postwar*, in which the European social model had been a beacon to the world, turned to cassandrism in *Ill Fares the Land*, which saw the welfare state as disastrously eroded by rising inequality and declining public services. Judt focused chiefly on the US and UK, but made clear that not even Sweden, France, Germany or the Netherlands had been exempt from negative developments.[76] What explained this deterioration? Principally, Judt argued, it was the fault of the generation that had grown up under the post-war welfare state and had taken the security it gave them for granted, becoming disaffected instead of grateful: 'the narcissism of the student movements,

---

[75] *Ill Fares the Land*, p. 142.
[76] *Ill Fares the Land*, pp. 113; 234.

new Left ideologues and the popular culture of the 60s generation invited a conservative backlash', allowing the Right to roll forward the 'intellectual revolution' mounted by Hayek and Friedman, imposing a free-market dogmatics on the political scene—an outcome that was 'far from inevitable'.[77]

For Judt, the crisis of the welfare state was therefore largely a matter of ideas—selfish ones on the part of the 60s radicals, and counter-arguments that were 'forceful indeed' from the Hayekians.[78] If things had been otherwise, the post-war consensus would presumably still be intact. What was striking was the complete absence of any economic explanation of the crisis in the 'Keynesian consensus' around Judt's welfare state. Where economic changes received any mention, it was always as an aside. Thus: 'As the post-war boom wound down'—no explanation of why it did so—unemployment rose and the tax-base of the state was threatened. Or: 'Only when the welfare state began to run into difficulties'—unexplained—did neo-liberal ideas take hold. Or: 'The growth in unemployment over the course of the 1970s' and 'the infla-tion of those years'—unexplained—put new strains on the exchequer.[79] Although the crisis of welfarism was the central topic in *Ill Fares the Land*, there was even less material explanation of it than in *Postwar*.

(iii) Social Democracy: success or failure?

Overlapping with Judt's account of welfarism was his depiction of the fate of social democracy, tacitly understood as parties of the Socialist International. Were they the vehicle for a renewed welfare state? Judt men-tioned in passing a variety of partly contradictory causes for their 'loss of nerve': a shrinking working class; the fall of Communism; the fact that social democracy 'in one form or another' had become so generalized—'the prose of contemporary European politics', as above—that the parties themselves now had little distinctive to offer.[80] But Judt could not afford to let such gloomy reflections go too far, lest they undermine the pur-pose of his book—a ringing call to revive social democracy as the last best hope of the age. The resulting sermon contradicted itself at every step. Thus, by the end of the twentieth century, social democracy had not

[77] *Ill Fares the Land*, pp. 83–4; 94–6.
[78] *Ill Fares the Land*, p. 97.
[79] *Ill Fares the Land*, pp. 79; 102; 147.
[80] *Ill Fares the Land*, pp. 86; 151; 143–4.

merely 'fulfilled many of its long-standing objectives', but 'succeeded beyond the wildest dreams of its founders'—though presumably Judt was not here referring to Marx, Engels, Bebel, Bernstein. Yet in that case, why was the land faring so ill? Or again: a 'defensive stance made sense' for social democracy, to 'convince voters that it was a respectable radical choice within a liberal polity'. Yet 'social democracy cannot just be about preserving worthy institutions as a defence against worse options'.[81]

(iv) What is to be done?

Success or failure, however, for the moment social democracy had 'lost its way'. What was needed to put it back on the right track? Judt's answer was a *ne plus ultra* of vapid idealism: it was a better kind of language that would change the world. For the problem of contemporary social democracy was 'not what to do' [*sic*] but 'how to talk about it'—'our disability is *discursive*: we simply do not know how to talk about these things any more'. *Ill Fares the Land* harped on this theme from the start, as Judt pondered how to answer a twelve-year-old who had warned him that the word 'socialism' was toxic in the US; Judt's solution was to tell the boy to forget 'socialism' and think instead of 'social democracy', with its wholesome 'acceptance of capitalism'.[82]

A 'new language of politics' was, of course, the thesis of Furet's *Rethinking the French Revolution*, in which society more or less levitated by the sheer magic of words. But Judt gave a characteristically British twist to this French conception: the discourse that would rescue social democracy was a 'moral narrative', though Judt did not explain what such a narrative might say. Combined with this was a call to rehabilitate the state, as 'the only institution standing between individuals and non-state actors like banks or international corporations'—though since Judt did not specify what the state should do, the effect was little more than rhetorical.[83] Judt was, of course, very ill at the time. Nevertheless, it boggles the mind to think that a serious observer of current affairs living in the United States could in 2010 describe the 'state' as a neutral third party, standing between banks and individuals. This was the political order that socialized the massive bank losses of 2008 against widespread popular rage. The discontinuity of style and personnel between Bush and Obama

---

[81] *Ill Fares the Land*, pp. 147; 229; 143; 233.
[82] *Ill Fares the Land*, pp. 6; 161; 234; 34; 229.
[83] *Ill Fares the Land*, p. 196; 183.

has only underscored the fundamental continuity of state policy toward the banks. *Ill Fares the Land* concluded with a desperately bland set of political prescriptions. 'Incremental improvements upon unsatisfactory circumstances are the best we can hope for, and all we should seek.'[84] With full allowance made for the conditions in which he was working at this stage—the nightmare of his advancing paralysis vividly described in the pages of the NYRB[85]—in Judt's final testament, neo-social democracy remains remarkably insipid.

Assessment

How do the accolades for Judt as a 'great historian', 'fearless critic' and 'brilliant political commentator' stand up against a cool examination of his work? As historiography, even his earliest, most substantial scholarly works on France—*Reconstruction of the Socialist Party* and *Socialism in Provence*—were weakened by the aggressive tendentiousness of his approach. *Marxism and the French Left* and *Past Imperfect* were avowedly selective and polemical. Judt lacked the most basic requirement for any student of intellectual history: the ability to grasp and reconstruct an idea with philological precision. His lack of interest in ideas is borne out *in extenso* throughout his copious writings on intellectuals: there were never any serious attempts to reconstruct a thinker's position, so as to probe and question it. Even summaries of figures to whom he was well-disposed were slapdash; writers to whom he was hostile were regularly excoriated for views they did not hold. Judged as an intellectual historian, the verdict on Judt must be negative. His magnum opus, *Postwar*, is regularly listed for undergraduate European History courses. But its 900 pages produced little new by way of evidence or interpretation—a weakness underlined by the absence of even the most minimal scholarly apparatus, beyond a 'general bibliography' available from NYU.

Judt himself confessed in his final interview that at school he had been considered 'better at literature than history'; also bragging, 'I was—and knew I was—among the best speakers and writers of my age cohort. I don't mean I was the best historian'.[86] In effect, it was his talent, limited but real, as a polemicist and a pamphleteer that disqualified Judt

---

[84] *Ill Fares the Land*, pp. 183; 224.
[85] Judt, 'Night', NYRB; collected, together with two dozen other short pieces, in *The Memory Chalet*.
[86] *Prospect*, August 2010.

as a historian of ideas, much as he liked to claim the loftier calling. His range as a polemicist was relatively narrow: there is a limit to what can be got from attacking the French left or lauding fellow defenders of the Free World. His negative judgements on political leaders—Thatcher, Bush, Clinton, Blair—carried little analytical heft; his belated criticism of Israel's West Bank settlements never explained at what point the Zionist project had gone wrong. Nevertheless, judged as a polemicist, the verdict can be more favourable, exonerating Judt of the heedless inconsistencies, both conceptual and analytic, that marred his work as historian of Europe and latter-day champion of neo-social democracy. A pamphleteer may be allowed—even expected—to change his views more or less at the drop of a hat. If the EU is now a moral beacon to the world, now a sad example of failed leadership; or the welfare state now the legacy of organized labour, now the common sense of capitalist politicians—so what? All grist to the mill. A historian will be held to different standards.

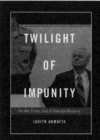

Twilight of Impunity
The War Crimes Trial of Slobodan Milosevic
JUDITH ARMATTA
576 pages, 15 illustrations, hardcover, $39.95

The Jacqueline Rose Reader
JACQUELINE ROSE
EDITED AND WITH AN INTRODUCTION BY
JUSTIN CLEMENS AND **BEN NAPARSTEK**
440 pages, 5 illustrations, paper, $25.95

Che's Travels
The Making of a Revolutionary
in 1950s Latin America
PAULO DRINOT, EDITOR
320 pages, 6 illustrations, paper, $23.95

A World of Becoming
WILLIAM E. CONNOLLY
A John Hope Franklin Center Book
224 pages, 3 photographs, paper, $22.95

Mao Zedong and China in the Twentieth-Century World
A Concise History
REBECCA E. KARL
Asia-Pacific: Culture, Politics, and Society
216 pages, paper, $21.95

Immanuel Wallerstein and the Problem of the World
System, Scale, Culture
DAVID PALUMBO-LIU, BRUCE ROBBINS,
AND **NIRVANA TANOUKHI,** EDITORS
272 pages, 18 illustrations, paper, $23.95

THE MAKING OF NEW WORLDS

Terrifying Muslims
Race and Labor in the South Asian Diaspora
JUNAID RANA
240 pages, 8 illustrations, paper, $23.95

Life Within Limits
Well-being in a World of Want
MICHAEL JACKSON
248 pages, 20 b&w photographs, paper, $22.95

Violence in a Time of Liberation
Murder and Ethnicity at a
South African Gold Mine, 1994
DONALD L. DONHAM
WITH PHOTOGRAPHS BY SANTU MOFOKENG
256 pages, 50 b&w photographs, paper, $22.95

A Foreigner Carrying in the Crook of His Arm a Tiny Bomb
AMITAVA KUMAR
232 pages, 13 photographs, paper, $21.95

DUKE
UNIVERSITY PRESS
www.dukepress.edu

In the U.K contact
Combined Academic Publishers
www.combinedacademic.co.uk

WILLIAM DAVIES

THE POLITICAL ECONOMY

OF UNHAPPINESS

F
OR THE MAJORITY of its history, Britain's National Health
Service has scarcely ever considered the specific health needs
of working people, other than those of its own staff. Almost
by definition, the NHS was originally dedicated to supporting
people who were outside of the labour market—new mothers, children,
the sick, the elderly and the dying. British doctors issued 'sick notes', cer-
tificates that were given to patients, informing their employers that they
were unable to work. But in recent years policy-makers have begun to
challenge these assumptions, along with the binary split between health
and illness, economically productive and economically needy, on which
they rested. In 2008, a review of the health of Britain's working-age
population was published jointly by the Department of Health and the
Department of Work and Pensions. Most strikingly, it calculated that the
annual cost to the British economy of health-related absence from work
was £100bn, only around £15bn less than the entire cost of the NHS.[1]

'Wellbeing' provides the policy paradigm by which mind and body can
be assessed as economic resources, with varying levels of health and productivity. In place of the binary split between the productive and the sick,
it offers gradations of economic, biological and psychological wellness.
And in place of a Cartesian dualism between tasks of the body and those
of the mind, blue and white collar, proponents of 'wellbeing' understand
the optimization of mind and body as amenable to a single, integrated
strategy. One of the leading influences on the UK government's work and
wellbeing programme, Gordon Waddell, is an orthopaedic surgeon whose
book *The Back Pain Revolution* helped transform policy perspectives on
work and health. Contrary to traditional medical assumptions—that 'rest
and recuperation' are the best means of getting the sick back to work—

Waddell argued that, in the case of back pain, individuals could recover better and faster if they stayed on the job.

Waddell's findings suggested that, even where work is primarily physical, medical and economic orthodoxy had underestimated the importance of psychological factors in determining health and productivity. Being at work has the psychological effect of making people believe themselves to be well, which in turn has a positive effect on their physical wellbeing. Hardt and Negri argue that, while 'immaterial' or 'cognitive' labour still only accounts for a small proportion of employment in quantitative terms, it has nevertheless become the *hegemonic* form of labour, serving 'as a vortex that gradually transforms other figures to adopt its central qualities'.[2] Waddell's work is a case of this transformation in action. The emerging alliance between economic policy-makers and health professionals is generating a new consensus, in which the psychological and 'immaterial' aspect of work and illness is what requires governing and optimizing, even for traditional manual labour. In place of the sick note, a new 'fit note' was introduced in 2010, enabling doctors to specify the positive physical and mental capabilities that a patient-employee still possessed and which an employer could still put to use.

There was another, more urgent reason for the new policy paradigm. As labour has become more 'immaterial', so has the nature of health-related absence from work. Some £30–40bn of the annual £100bn lost to the UK economy through health-related absence was due to mental-health disorders.[3] Around a million people in the UK are claiming incapacity benefit due to depression and anxiety.[4] Figure 1 indicates the gradual 'dematerialization' of incapacity over recent years. The turn towards 'wellbeing', as a bio-psycho-social capacity, enables employers and healthcare professionals to recognize the emotional and psychological problems that inhibit work, but also to develop techniques for getting employees to improve their wellbeing and productive potential. Even more than back pain, mental illness is considered to be better treated by keeping people in work, than absenting them from it. In contrast to

---

[1] Health, Work and Well-being Programme, *Working for a Healthier Tomorrow: Dame Carol Black's Review of the Health of the Working Age Population*, London 2008.
[2] Michael Hardt and Antonio Negri, *Multitude: War and Democracy in the Age of Empire*, London 2004, p. 107.
[3] UK DWP, *Working Our Way to Better Mental Health*, 2008.
[4] Richard Layard et al, 'Cost-Benefit Analysis of Psychological Therapy', *National Institute Economic Review*, vol. 202, no. 1, 2007.

FIGURE I. *Incapacity-benefits claimants by primary medical condition*

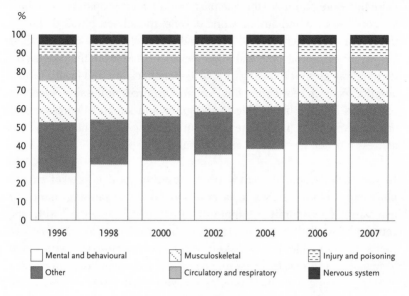

Source: DWP Administrative Data.

a neo-classical or utilitarian perspective, which would treat work as the opposite of utility, many economists also now argue that work is a positive force for mental health, and that unemployment causes suffering out of any proportion to the associated loss of earnings.

Depressive hegemony

Depression is the iconic illness in this respect. Indeed, we might say that if 'immaterial' labour is now the hegemonic form of production, depression is the hegemonic form of incapacity. Typically, depression is characterized by a lack of any clear clinical definition; indeed it is often defined as anything that can be treated with anti-depressants.[5] Depression is just *sheer incapacity*, a distinctly neo-liberal form of psychological deficiency, representing the flipside of an ethos that implores individuals to act, enjoy, perform, create, achieve and maximize. In an economy based in large part on services, enthusiasm, dynamism and optimism are vital workplace resources. The depressed employee is stricken by a chronic deflation of these psycho-economic capacities, which can lead him or her

---

[5] Alain Ehrenberg, *The Weariness of the Self: Diagnosing the History of Depression in the Contemporary Age*, Montreal 2008.

to feel economically useless, and consequently more depressed. The work-place therefore acquires a therapeutic function, for if people can somehow be persuaded to remain in work despite mental or physical illness, then their self-esteem will be prevented from falling too low, and their bio-psycho-economic potential might be rescued. Many of the UK govern-ment's strategies for reducing incapacity-benefit claims and health-related absence focus on reorienting the Human Resources profession, such that managers become better able to recognize and support depressed and anxious employees. Lifting the taboo surrounding mental illness, so as to address it better, has become an economic-policy priority.

In the early 1990s, the study of the psychological effects of unem-ployment was the catalyst for a new and rapidly expanding branch of neo-classical economics: happiness economics.[6] Together with the concept of wellbeing, happiness—sometimes referred to as 'subjective wellbeing'—provides policy-makers with a new analytical tool with which to measure and govern economic agents. It represents one prominent attempt to cope with the 'crisis of measure' that arises when capital-ism's principal resources and outputs are no longer solely physical, yet still require economic quantification in order to be valued. At an aggre-gate level, concern for the happiness of entire nations, and the failure of economic growth to improve it, has inspired political leaders to demand new official 'indicators' of social and economic progress, which account for this intangible psychological entity. President Sarkozy's 'Stiglitz Commission' on the measurement of national progress made headlines around the world, while the Australian, American and British statistical agencies are already collecting official data to track national happiness levels.[7] The gap between growth in material and psychological prosperity, known as 'Easterlin's Paradox' after a 1974 article on this topic by econo-mist Richard Easterlin, is soon to receive official endorsement.[8]

Unhappiness has become the critical negative externality of con-temporary capitalism. In addition to the policy interventions already mentioned, the New Labour government introduced an Increasing

---

[6] The seminal article was Andrew Oswald and Andrew Clark, 'Unhappiness and Unemployment', *Economic Journal*, vol. 104, no. 424, 1994.
[7] Jean-Paul Fitoussi, Amartya Sen and Joseph Stiglitz, *Report of the Commission on the Measurement of Economic Performance and Social Progress*, 2009.
[8] Richard Easterlin, 'Does Economic Growth Improve the Human Lot?' in Paul David and Melvin Reder, eds, *Nations and Households in Economic Growth: Essays in Honor of Moses Abramovitz*, New York 1974.

Access to Psychological Therapies (IAPT) programme, to make Cognitive Behavioural Therapy more widely available via the NHS. Richard Layard, an economist at the London School of Economics appointed by Blair as the UK's 'happiness tsar', stressed the economic significance of this programme, urging that it be expanded further in response to rising unemployment. The sheer *inefficiency* of depression, and the efficiency of CBT in tackling it, is demonstrated by Layard in a paper making the 'business case' for spending more public money on talking cures.[9] CBT, and policy enthusiasm for it, is controversial amongst psychotherapists and psychologists, many of whom view it as a 'sticking plaster' which conceals mental illness, at best for limited periods of time.[10] Yet, by virtue of being clearly time-limited—a course of CBT can last a mere six sessions—and output-oriented, it is amenable to an economic calculus in a way that traditional psychoanalysis or psychotherapy are patently not. Programmes for getting unemployed people back to work in the UK now offer CBT courses, in an effort to re-inflate their desire to overcome economic odds.

Thinking pleasure

Optimistic theorists of cognitive capitalism, such as Hardt and Negri, believe that the positive externalities or spill-over effects associated with immaterial production create the conditions for a new commons. Efforts to measure and privatize human, intellectual and cultural resources must ultimately fail; the hegemonic character of immaterial labour means that the most valuable economic resources are becoming socialized, despite the best efforts of capital to prevent this. The proposition I wish to investigate here is in some ways the inverse: while policy-makers, doctors and economists seek to contain the negative externality of unhappiness as a measurable psychological deficiency and economic cost, it has inherently political and sociological qualities that lend it critical potential. One contradiction of neo-liberalism is that it demands levels of enthusiasm, energy and hope whose conditions it destroys through insecurity, powerlessness and the valorization of unattainable ego ideals via advertising. What is most intriguing about the turn towards happiness amongst political elites and orthodox economists is that it is bringing this truth to the fore, and granting it official statistical endorsement. Even a cursory

---

[9] Layard et al, 'Cost-Benefit Analysis'.
[10] See Oliver James, 'Therapy on the NHS? What a Crazy Waste of £600m!', *Daily Mail*, 24 October 2006.

examination of the evidence on unhappiness in neo-liberal societies draws the observer beyond the limits of psychology, and into questions of political economy.

For heuristic purposes, let us grant that the terms 'happiness' and 'unhappiness' can be conceptualized in three different registers. The first is merely mental and utilitarian, where 'happiness' is primarily understood as the immediate experience of pleasure, or *hedonia*. 'Unhappiness' would therefore refer to some breakdown of consumer choice, personal relationships or neuro-chemical processes, with depression becoming a proxy for these. The second is ethical and teleological, where 'happiness' is understood as the attainment of a good life, or *eudaimonia*. Within this register, 'unhappiness' represents a lack of positive capability to act meaningfully in pursuit of one's own substantive goals; unhappiness, from this perspective, would be akin to what republican thinkers term subjection to 'domination'. And the third is historical and messianic, the endlessly delayed promise of Enlightenment. This is the tragic teleology of the Frankfurt School, whereby we experience the possibility of happiness via its apparently perpetual absence, but—like Kant—must retain some distant faith in a collective human *telos*, if only because critique is impossible without it.

To the extent that these different registers can be kept ontologically separate, the emerging regime of wellbeing policies and measurement can successfully contain unhappiness as a neuro-psycho-economic phenomenon. And yet, as the recent statistical interest in social and economic 'progress' suggests, the neo-classical discourse surrounding happiness and unhappiness invariably strays into ethical, then teleological, and then critical terrain. On the one hand this leads to an instrumentalization of critical, ethical and Enlightenment concerns (as the *measurement* of historical progress would suggest); but on the other, the contradictions and injuries of neo-liberal capitalism start to show up within the very positivist bodies of knowledge that are intended to regulate and sustain it. If the 'need to lend a voice to suffering is a condition of all truth', perhaps liberal economics is on the verge of uncovering truths that it never previously imagined.[11]

Capitalism would seem to require an optimal balance of happiness and unhappiness amongst its participants, if it is to be sustainable. The need

---

[11] Theodor Adorno, *Negative Dialectics*, London 1973, pp. 17–18.

for *dissatisfaction* is implicitly recognized by Keynesian economics, which sees the capitalist system as threatened by the possibility of individual or collective satisfaction, manifest as a demand shortfall. Capitalism's gravest problem is then how to maintain governments or consumers in a state of dissatisfied hunger, and how to find ever more credit through which to feed that hunger. The defining difference between the Keynesian era and the neo-liberal era was simply that the former depended on an insatiable, debt-fuelled, 'unhappy' state, whereas the latter depended on an insatiable, debt-fuelled, 'unhappy' consumer. The question of who or what is to inject such an appetite in future has no apparent answer as yet.

Max Weber, and more recently Luc Boltanski and Eve Chiapello in *The New Spirit of Capitalism*, addressed a parallel problem, but via moral and cultural sociology. To what extent and on what basis must capitalism serve our human needs and desires, if we are to remain committed to it? Immaterial needs and desires play a key role, as these are less easily exhaustible than material ones. As Boltanski and Chiapello argue:

> Whereas capitalism, by its very nature, is an insatiable process, people are satiable, so that they require justifications for getting involved in an insatiable process. It follows that capitalism cannot make do with offering nothing more specific than its inherent insatiability.

The culture of capitalism must keep individuals sufficiently dissatisfied that they continue to seek satisfaction from it, but not so dissatisfied that they reject or resist it outright. Boltanski and Chiapello's central argument is that capitalism has drawn on varieties of anti-capitalist critique in generating the 'spirit' which induces a sufficient mass of the population to remain at this finely tuned level of engagement. At key moments of crisis, capitalist accumulation has alternately drawn on those criticizing its unfairness (the 'social critique') and those criticizing its dullness (the 'artistic critique') in order to find 'routes to its own survival'.[12] In promising to answer these critics, it pledges to treat the moral and human injuries that it itself has enacted, thereby renewing its legitimacy.

The spirit of capitalism regulates the political economy of unhappiness, aiming to ensure that individuals find partial fulfilment in work and consumption. If they found no fulfilment, there would be a risk that

---

[12] Luc Boltanski and Eve Chiapello, *The New Spirit of Capitalism*, London and New York 2006, pp. 486; 27.

they might opt out; yet if they found too much fulfilment, this could signify a satisfaction of desire that is anathema to an economic system that depends on desire remaining inexhaustible. Real happiness, Adorno reminds us, would mean no longer seeking ever more and ever newer sources of satisfaction. Real progress would mean abandoning the obsession with technical and economic progress. Far safer, therefore, for the capitalist to promise substantive *eudaimonia*, but to deliver only a taste of it, or substitute it for a more instant *hedonic* experience that leaves the individual still wanting more. During periods of stability, capitalism successfully regulates this distribution of happiness and unhappiness. That unhappiness is now appearing as a costly and threatening negative externality to be tackled by the state suggests that this equilibrium is breaking down.

Industrial psychology

Boltanski and Chiapello examine the 'new spirit of capitalism' via human-resource management texts which, as they point out, must go beyond the narrow prescriptions of neo-classical economics and argue for more than the pursuit of efficiency and profit. From Hugo Munsterburg's 1912 *Psychology and Industrial Efficiency* onwards, management theory has depended far more on the insights of applied psychology than on the harsh rationalism of Taylorism or economics.[13] Human Resource Management emerged from the industrial psychology studies of Elton Mayo in the 1920s, developed via the famous Hawthorne experiments of the 1930s, and expanded under the influence of the psychologist Kurt Lewin in the post-war period to engage with theories of group behaviour, as explored by Lewin and the Tavistock Institute during the 1950s.[14] The discourse of management theory is, strikingly, both instrumentalist and moral. It is instrumentalist inasmuch as it self-evidently exists to serve the interests of managers and those 'principals' on whose behalf management acts, namely the owners of capital. But it is moral inasmuch as

---

[13] Frederick Taylor himself was of course an engineer, not a psychologist, and his *Principles of Scientific Management* (1911) consequently offers little to the employer concerned with motivation and morale.
[14] See Loren Baritz, *The Servants of Power: A History of the Use of Social Science in American Industry*, New York 1960; Stephen Barley and Gideon Kunder, 'Design and Devotion: Surges of Rational and Normative Ideologies of Control in Managerial Discourse', *Administrative Science Quarterly*, vol. 37, no. 3, 1992; Peter Miller and Nikolas Rose, 'The Tavistock Programme: The Government of Subjectivity and Social Life', *Sociology*, vol. 22, no. 2, 1988.

it takes seriously the need for happiness, respect, engagement and community, at least within groups. This morality is not a complete sham. Rather, instrumental and substantive reason are wedded together in psychological concepts such as 'teamwork' and 'leadership', whereby employees are viewed as morally endowed, emotional beings to be mobilized and co-operated with.

Advertising is no less important in producing and regulating the new spirit of capitalism. It too conducts a subtle game of instrumentalizing unhappiness and dissatisfaction with capitalism as a motivation for consumption. This was witnessed as early as the 1920s, when American marketers targeted a growing collective sense of *ennui* and alienation from urban-capitalist existence, a feeling that more innocent, dependable relations were being lost. The images used to sell products during the 1920s and 30s were specifically drawn from a social ideal of traditional family and community life that industrial capitalism appeared to be destroying.[15] By the 1960s, advertising was tapping into frustrations with bourgeois and bureaucratic routines, speaking to the counter-culture even as it was first emerging.[16] Advertising, like management theory, is fuelled by a critique of the dominant normative-economic regime within which it sits, facilitating safe acts of micro-rebellion against the macro-social order. It acts as capital's own trusted moral and artistic critic in order to inspire additional psychological engagement on the part of ordinary worker-consumers. Dissatisfaction is reduced to a psychological tendency to be fed back into processes of production and consumption. As a result, understanding such psychological qualities as impulse, libido and frustration—often in the micro-social context of the 'focus group'—has been key to the development of advertising since the 1920s.

As tools of economic administration and legitimation, neo-classical economics and psychology have had a relatively clear, yet mutually supportive, division of labour since their split at the start of the twentieth century. The pioneering economists of the 1870s and 80s did engage with questions regarding psychological states, as it was in the subjective experience of happiness that they placed their concept of value, in contrast to

---

[15] See Stuart Ewen, *Captains of Consciousness: Advertising and the Social Roots of Consumer Culture*, New York 1976.
[16] Thomas Frank, *The Conquest of Cool: Business Culture, Counter-culture and the Rise of Hip Consumerism*, Chicago 1998.

the labour theory of value of classical political economy. In 1881, Francis Edgeworth even went as far as proposing the creation of a 'hedonimeter', a measurement device that would gauge levels of mental pleasure as the basis of a new economic science.[17] But after Marshall and Pareto had distanced themselves from this largely speculative concern with the psyche, and with psychologists developing experimental techniques in the late 1890s, neo-classical economics cut itself off from any empirical concern with the mind. It opted instead to study preferences via choice-making behaviour, on the methodological presupposition that this was a perfect representation of how pleasure and pain were experienced.

This formal premise, often referred to as *homo economicus*, enabled a clean split between neo-classical economics and empirical psychology that lasted for most of the twentieth century. The mental realm—like the social realm, which was also acquiring its own specialist branch of social science—would be external to the territory of neo-classical economics. Economics could thereby focus purely on questions of rational choice and efficiency, leaving the study of irrational behaviour and 'equity' to the rival social sciences of psychology and sociology. Not least, it helped to define what counted as 'economic' in the first place, through designating the limits of market logic. Neo-classical economics was an adamantly amoral, rationalist science, which could be employed as a neutral tool to regulate and delineate markets, but did not recognize happiness or unhappiness as anything other than a calculable, utilitarian phenomenon, subject to a logic of price. Similarly, any assessment of social or political action would be on efficiency grounds alone, or what following Arthur Pigou became known as 'market failure' grounds. Chicago economists, led by Gary Becker and Ronald Coase, later went further still in establishing efficiency explanations for various 'social' and 'normative' institutions and practices, such as marriage, law and firms.

The mind and its injuries are now being brought within the purview of mainstream economics and subject to an efficiency analysis. The implication of the wellbeing policy agenda is that dynamics of happiness and unhappiness, satisfaction and dissatisfaction, can no longer be left in the hands of applied psychologists and their colleagues in management and marketing. Neo-classical economics has hitherto avoided

---

[17] David Colander, 'Edgeworth's Hedonimeter and the Quest to Measure Utility', *Journal of Economic Perspectives*, vol. 21, no. 2, Spring 2007.

directly confronting the 'immaterial' nature of Western post-industrial capitalism, disguising it with the metaphor of 'human capital', which treats the mind as analogous to physical fixed capital, such as machinery. But persistent, stultifying unhappiness represents a form of negativity that can neither be contained within the psychological techniques of marketing and management, nor explained within the rationalist logic of inadequate 'human capital' investment. Negativity, primarily in the form of depression, is being confronted at a societal level as a bio-psychological epidemic that undermines the viability of post-industrial capitalism.

To respond to this particular crisis of measure, economics and psychology are being forcibly re-married. Behavioural and experimental economics have their earliest origins in game theory in the 1940s, which allowed economists and psychologists to compare normative rational choice-making—that is, according to neo-classical economics—with empirical choice-making, as observed under laboratory conditions. The gap between economists' prescriptions for how people should behave and what they actually do became subject to testing. Discovering patterns in such 'anomalies' became the preoccupation of behavioural economists, following Kahneman and Tversky's landmark 1979 article on 'prospect theory', which later won them a Nobel Prize.[18]

The economic study of happiness has different antecedents, but led in a similar direction. Hadley Cantril's 1965 *The Pattern of Human Concerns* represents the first attempt to measure and compare the happiness of entire nations, and provided much of the data used by Easterlin in his 1974 article comparing GDP growth with happiness growth. The late 1960s also witnessed the birth of the positive psychology movement, focused on psychological optimization rather than normalization, and the birth of the social indicators movement, which sought to measure various intangible socio-economic assets, including wellbeing. Psychologists came to enquire into sources of happiness for the first time, developing new scales and questionnaires with which to do so, while social-indicators researchers employed survey techniques and questionnaires to measure immaterial assets, informal interactions and quality of life. This coincided with an emerging awareness of depression as a mental affliction, challenging the techniques of psychoanalysis

---

[18] Daniel Kahneman and Amos Tversky, 'Prospect Theory: An Analysis of Decision Under Risk', *Econometrica*, vol. 47, no. 2, 1979.

that had been developed principally to relieve patients of neuroses and feelings of guilt. Depression, by contrast, necessitated techniques for mental reactivation, which CBT, a derivative of positive psychology, now promised to deliver.

Thanks to the new empirical techniques and data sets, economists could start to spot anomalies—cases where human happiness does not rise and fall as neo-classical economics would predict. At the centre of happiness economics sits the psychological concept of 'adaptation', the extent to which individuals do or do not become psychologically attuned to changes in their circumstances. Where they do adapt to changed circumstances—for example, of increased monetary income or national wealth—their happiness ceases to correspond to changed objective conditions, at least after the transition has passed. Where they do *not* adapt to changed circumstances—as with unemployment—their happiness remains directly proportionate to their objective conditions, regardless of how long they have lived with them.

Happiness economics took off during the 1990s, drawing on data provided by a number of national household surveys, which had included questions on 'subjective wellbeing' from 1984 onwards. With it has come the rise of *homo psycho-economicus*, a form of economic subjectivity in which choice-making is occasionally misguided, emotional or subject to social and moral influences. If *homo economicus* was unhappy, that was merely because he had insufficient money or consumer choice. But *homo psycho-economicus* suffers from psychological afflictions as well. He makes mistakes because he follows others too instinctively; he consumes things which damage his health, relationships and environment; he sometimes becomes unhappy—or even happy—out of all proportion to his material circumstances.[19]

Regulating wellness

Homo psycho-economicus is less rational, less calculating, than *homo economicus*; but to what extent is he a social creature? Wellbeing policies

[19] The field of neuro-economics is expanding rapidly, convincing some economists that the question of what truly makes people happy and unhappy will soon be placed on an objective footing, no longer requiring surveys at all. See for example Richard Layard, *Happiness: Lessons from a New Science*, London 2005.

can be seen as efforts to get people to conform more closely to the ideal of neo-classical rationality, and the 'Robinson Crusoe' rugged individualism that it assumes. But the re-engagement with psychology eventually necessitates the rediscovery of sociability, if only via the importance of groups, therapy and psychological norms. Service-sector capitalism draws precisely on those innate human capabilities—sociability, mental activity, creativity, communication—that neo-classical economics had treated as 'externalities'; hence the 'non-economic' becomes more valuable than the 'economic' (narrowly understood).

What is new today is that the state is now stepping in to confront psychological problems of motivation and dissatisfaction that were previously the concern of management and HR professionals.[20] The NHS is being mobilized to increase the bio-psychological potency of the working-age population, not as a social 'externality' to the labour market, as embodied by the sick note, but as an asset within it, as certified by the 'fit note'. 'Nudging' individuals to take 'better' decisions for their bodies, old age, environments and families—as prescribed by *Nudge*, a best-selling work of behavioural economics, allegedly required reading for Cameron's coalition Cabinet—has become a policy strategy for aligning psychological impulses with longer-term economic efficiency.[21] Again, rather than treat problems such as obesity, economic insecurity, environmental degradation and bad parenting as social, normative or psychological issues that are beyond the limits of markets and economics, the emerging economic logic treats them as inefficiencies that can be dealt with through better management of consumer choice. Competition regulators are now importing lessons from behavioural economics, to ensure that the 'choice architectures' presented to consumers do not imperil their capacity to take the 'right' decision. This is a significant disavowal of the Hayekian, neo-liberal model of the state, that focused on creating the market conditions within which diverse consumer preferences could be pursued as efficiently as possible.

---

[20] The HR profession is also taking on healthcare responsibilities that were previously the preserve of the state. More employers now offer gym membership, physiotherapy, smoking-cessation programmes and even psychological counselling, as part of their own 'wellbeing' programmes. See *Building the Case for Wellness*, PriceWaterhouseCoopers, 2008.
[21] Richard Thaler and Cass Sunstein, *Nudge: Improving Decisions about Health, Wealth and Happiness*, New Haven 2008.

In an age when the most valuable assets and products are intangible and cognitive, accounting techniques have to somehow include capacities to think, feel and communicate. Minds must be measured, valued and invested in, even if this means opening up economics to the possibility that people are 'irrational', social and moral creatures. After all, their sociability and morality may also yield satisfactory investment returns. Future policy proposals include teaching happiness or 'resilience' skills in schools, while 'voluntary' forms of sociability and gift-giving are now also internal to a governing economic logic, as the British government's prioritization of 'The Big Society'—a neo-communitarian policy programme aimed at increasing non-market exchange—now indicates.

The ambiguity that lurks within this emerging apparatus of government is that between the *hedonic* and the *eudaimonic* registers of happiness. The failure of neo-classical economics, and of neo-liberal regulation generally, stems from its excessive commitment to hedonism, the utility form of pleasure. The neo-classical assumption—enshrined in neo-liberal regulatory agencies—that economic agents are incapable of making a 'bad' choice, has hit multiple crises, most graphically in the case of financial markets, where the quest for psychological kicks is held culpable for bringing down entire banks. But it is also increasingly apparent that insatiable consumption can undermine the potential for mental wellbeing, and be entirely compatible with depression. Mark Fisher captures this neo-liberal paradox of happiness in his portrait of students he once taught at a further education college:

> Many of the teenage students I encountered seemed to be in a state of what I would call depressive hedonia. Depression is usually characterized as a state of anhedonia, but the condition I'm referring to is constituted not by an inability to get pleasure so much as by an inability to do anything else except pursue pleasure. There is a sense that 'something is missing'— but no appreciation that this mysterious, missing enjoyment can only be accessed beyond the pleasure principle.[22]

The Weberian insight that capitalism cannot sustain itself only by offering more money, more choice and more pleasure, is at the heart of this crisis. The 'spirit' of capitalism is its promise of not only utility or *hedonia*, but also of meaning or *eudaimonia*; not simply psychological-economic gratification, but a form of ethical fulfilment and the demonstration of

---

[22] Mark Fisher, *Capitalist Realism: Is There No Alternative?*, Ropley 2009, pp. 21–2.

innate self-worth. If a regime of capitalism neglects the latter, it encounters a moral crisis. Managers and advertisers may have been attuned to this requirement for the best part of a century, but evidently they have now neglected their duties, and economic technocrats are coming to the rescue.

From ill-being to critique

In 2007, the British government's Department for Culture, Media and Sport was criticized in a cross-departmental 'Capability Review' carried out by the Cabinet Office for its poor economic evaluations and inadequate 'focus on outcomes', a problem it described as 'urgent'.[23] The difficulty for DCMS is that its output is largely public and intangible; it exists to generate positive externalities, in the form of creativity, cultural 'buzz' and sporting prowess. The Culture Minister duly hired a private-sector economics consultancy to perform an output evaluation, using a new public-accounting technique based on happiness economics.[24] The method, known as the 'income compensation' technique, poses the following question: how much private monetary income would be necessary to compensate a person psychologically for the loss of a specific public good that he or she can currently use for free? For example, if someone regularly visits a free public art gallery, their measured happiness levels may be x per cent higher than someone who does not do so. It is then possible to assess how much private income this x per cent difference corresponds to, using established data on the correlation between happiness and pay. That figure can then be multiplied by the number of households who visit the gallery in question, to produce an artificial proxy for its 'market price'. The same technique has been proposed for use by law courts in setting damages payments, where a claimant has suffered some emotional or psychological harm.[25]

The problem that this technique encounters, from a policy-maker's point of view, is that it ends up valuing public and non-market goods at implausibly high levels. Private income is such a weak correlate of

---

[23] Capabilities Review Team, *Capability Review for the Department of Culture, Media and Sport*, 2007.
[24] Department of Culture, Media and Sport, *Making the Case*, 2010.
[25] Andrew Oswald and Nattavudh Powdthavee, 'Death, Happiness and the Calculation of Compensatory Damages', in Eric Posner and Cass Sunstein, eds, *Law and Happiness*, Chicago 2010.

happiness, when compared to 'social' and public goods, that it often takes extraordinarily large monetary payments to compensate for the loss of non-market goods. The Department of Culture, Media and Sport study found that regular attendance of concerts had an impact on happiness equivalent to £9,000 of additional income. Elsewhere, studies have shown that an unemployed person would need an annual income of £250,000 to compensate for the psychological injury of not having a job.[27] Economists using the income-compensation technique are aware that it could potentially justify common ownership and planning of large swathes of the economy, on the technical basis that one pound spent collectively generates a far greater psycho-economic return on investment than the same pound spent privately. The political ramifications of such a technique have to be carefully concealed by the neo-classical economists currently seeking to introduce it to policy-making. But, arguably, a spectre is haunting liberal economics.

Human ill-being is never merely an absence of pleasure, which is one thing that consumer society can usually promise to avoid; nor is it even an absence of any substantive meaning, which the 'spirit' of capitalism can partially deliver on, if only as an epiphenomenon. Followed to its logical conclusion, it is an absence of democracy, and consequently a basis for resistance and critique. Happiness economics starts with a psychological interest in *hedonia* and the mind, strays into ethical questions of *eudaimonia* and society, and eventually grapples clumsily with the Kantian dilemma of Enlightenment—what is all this rationality, efficiency and technology ultimately for? The meaninglessness of utilitarianism, and the emptiness of hedonism, are now subject to empirical and statistical analysis. On the one hand, this is a co-option and subsumption of core Enlightenment and critical thinking, to rival—but exceed—the capacity of management and marketing discourse to internalize the critique of capitalism. To the pessimist, the fact that economists have discovered unhappiness and history may look like the final triumph of immanence. The optimistic reading would be that when positivists seek to grasp and quantify the immeasurable problem of unhappiness, they encounter causes of that unhappiness that are far larger than economic or medical policy can calculate or alleviate. Is it too much to hope that, if critique can be rendered psychological, then the reverse may also be true: that mental ill-being may be rendered critical?

---

[27] Nicola Bacon et al, *The State of Happiness*, London 2010.

NEW FROM VERSO

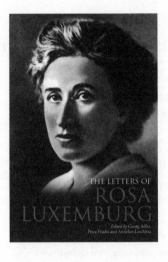

THE LETTERS OF ROSA LUXEMBURG

Edited by Annelies Laschitza,
Georg Adler and Peter Hudis

Translated by George Shriver

HB • $39.95/£25.99 • 978-1-84467-453-4

'The most comprehensive collection of her correspondence yet to appear in English. It transports us directly into the private world of a woman who has never lost her inspirational power as an original thinker and courageous activist.'—*Sheila Rowbotham, The Guardian*

'Perhaps for the first time in English, Rosa Luxemburg emerges whole from the shadows of Stalinism and previous biographers . . . A wonderfully compelling record, both poignant and timely.'—*The Observer*

'Rosa Luxemburg's letters have been published in English before, but this collection, of which about two-thirds are newly translated, has delivered to us a real, recognizable human being. In the previous volumes, Luxemburg often seemed uniformly heroic; here we have her in all her strength and all her frailty. She emerges as one of the most emotionally intelligent socialists in modern history.'—*Vivian Gornick, The Nation*

VERSO

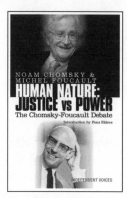

MARK ELVIN

CHINA'S

MULTIPLE REVOLUTIONS

HERE ARE MANY kinds of revolutions in human history: technological, demographic, economic, cultural, ideological, intellectual, political.* They overlap, intertwine and weave in and out of each other. In the course of the last two centuries, Chinese life as experienced by both ordinary and extraordinary people has been through all of these, often more than once, in a fascinating—sometimes terrifying—kaleidoscopic variety. People can and do refer to 'the' Chinese revolutions of 1911 and 1949, meaning in the main particular sequences of twentieth-century military and political events, and this is acceptable as shorthand. But perhaps the most effective way to acquire a feeling for these life-changing processes as a whole is to begin, not with the political on its own, or political events over a relatively brief space of time, but with the deeper changes in the imagined but emotionally powerful *stories* in terms of which people understand their lives, as a long-term phenomenon.[1]

The number of 'stories' in which the Chinese have been, so to speak, 'living' in modern times—believing and then disbelieving, preaching and then jettisoning them—has been remarkable. Just to illustrate, not one but *two* very different, elaborately articulated and government-sponsored systems of sacred-text-based, quasi-religious belief have been in effect abandoned by the Chinese in the course of four or five generations: the first was scriptural Confucianism, which ceased reproducing itself around the beginning of the twentieth century, when the imperial civil-service examinations were abolished; the second was the intellectually degraded but emotionally powerful simplification of Marxism by Mao and his think-tank of ideologues—Chen Boda, Ai Siqi—which did not really survive the end of the Cultural Revolution in the later 1970s.

And this is not to mention such short-lived florescences as the faith the Taiping rebels borrowed from the missionaries in the 1850s and early 1860s: 'Christianity with Chinese characteristics', as it might be described, and including toward its end a modernization programme. Or the well-intentioned but intellectually unconvincing attempt at a cult of Sun Yat-sen's thought (*Sanminzhuyi*) in Taiwan a century later. The period also saw parallel national-historical developments: the decline of China, as one of the four great Eurasian empires during the eighteenth century;[2] and then its mid-nineteenth-century humiliation by Western military forces—though *not*, as is sometimes implied by loose statements about 'imperialism', its general *conquest*, excluding limited foreign occupations of relatively small areas; there was never a foreign Viceroy in Nanjing, in contrast with the one in New Delhi under the British, and I doubt if there ever could have been. Decline has been followed in its turn by China's recent resurgence to be at least a potential future superpower.

This epoch was also the beginning of the gradual but extensive—and still continuing—transfer of most of the West's advanced technological skills into Chinese hands, starting seriously in the 1860s in Shanghai with ships and machinery.[3] The chemical fertilizers invented in Germany, following the discoveries of Justus von Liebig (1803–73), were the single most important aspect of this transfer, without which it would have become impossible for China to feed its swelling population of the later twentieth century. It also saw the arrival of modern science, the key transformative factor in the modern world, which had been missing in China before this time—apart from one or two isolated successes, and the marginal though analytically demanding field of reconstructing the ancient and medieval pronunciations of the Chinese

---

* This paper was first published in Chinese as a contribution to a symposium organized by the Taipei-based journal *Sixiang* [*Reflexion*], no. 18, June 2011.

[1] As Sartre has written, 'a man is always a teller of stories; he lives surrounded by his stories and the stories of others, and he perceives all that happens to him through these stories. And he seeks to live his life as if he were telling a story.' Jean-Paul Sartre, *La Nausée* (1938), Paris 1958, p. 57.

[2] See the map 'Competing Imperialisms in Eurasia' in Caroline Blunden and Mark Elvin, *Cultural Atlas of China*, New York 1998, pp. 34–5, showing the growth phases of the Qing-dynasty Chinese, Tsarist Russian, English Indian, and Ottoman territories.

[3] For the early part of this process, see Mark Elvin, 'Le transfert des technologies avant la seconde guerre mondiale', *Nouveaux Mondes* 2, Summer 1993.

language.[4] All of these phenomena were interwoven with politics, to varying degrees; but probably the only indispensable political aspect was the opening of the door to trade and diplomacy with the western world, in the 1840s and 1850s, by the two conventionally but inadequately labelled 'Opium Wars'.[5]

Some years ago, in *Changing Stories in the Chinese World*, I tried to show, mainly through extracts from five novels directly or indirectly about Chinese society in their period, and some Qing-dynasty poems on everyday life, how dramatically the Chinese experience of living and of understanding the world and its history, had changed since the 1820s.[6] Let us begin by sketching the socio-political world that we are considering through a summary of what this survey shows. The story is an intricate one.

Warning bells

The first novel is *The Destinies of the Flowers in the Mirror* (*Jinghua yuan*), by Li Ruzhen. Written in the years before 1828, it is a Chinese *Gulliver's Travels*, full of subtle humour, mocking—with a serious didactic intent beneath the laughter—the many pompous pretensions and foolish beliefs of Qing society, not to mention the self-satisfied inadequacies of too much of its scholarship. It also champions the case for women—and even, at times, the young and the non-Chinese—to be taken as seriously and treated as respectfully as men. At a deeper level it is a richly self-contradictory mix of unflinching belief in both the moral and ritual proprieties of Confucianism—notably, filial obedience and the self-denial of faithful widows—and the Buddhist-Daoist karmic justice of the unending reincarnation of human, animal and even spirit selves. Deeper still, Li Ruzhen holds that there is a predetermined web of causation that is forever largely unknowable to mortals, but 'the roots

---

[4] Mark Elvin, 'Some Reflections on the Use of "Styles of Scientific Thinking" to Disaggregate and Sharpen Comparisons between China and Europe from Song to Mid-Qing Times, 960–1850 CE', *History of Technology* 25, 2004.

[5] Several decades ago I read through items mentioning opium in the *Veritable Records of the Qing* (*Qing shilu*) for the 1830s, and found that, just *prior to* the first 'Opium War', references to the internal problems of the opium trade—China by then being a considerable producer of the drug—well outnumbered references to opium brought in from overseas. The British did not force opium on China, but sold—very profitably—to networks of Chinese dealers already well-established.

[6] Mark Elvin, *Changing Stories in the Chinese World*, Stanford 1998.

determine the blossoms, just as the magnet is drawn toward the iron'.[7] The novel has a knowledgeable fascination with technology, including accurate clocks (useful, among other things, for measuring the speed of sound), imagined flying machines, and the details of the engineering needed for the hydraulic control of waterways. It is also haunted by a sense of the gap between the ideal and the actual. China is seen as undoubtedly 'the root of all other countries', but unfortunately a flawed one that needs improvement.[8] The universe is run by a celestial bureaucracy of lesser gods and spirits under the Lord on High (shangdi), but one as much riven with vicious personal rivalries and imperfections as its human counterpart on earth. But, crucially, China was believed to be at the heart of all that mattered, whether in human history or human ideas—a belief that was to be largely in ruins a hundred years later. The loss of this comforting delusion created an agonizing nostalgia for a past which was indeed great—but not uniquely great—that has not, even today, been completely laid to rest.

This was something of an elitist vision. Almost none of the common people could speak for themselves directly in our historical sources. But there were many poets—some of them of modest origins, though, through their sophisticated literacy, real or virtual members of the 'gentry' class—who were acutely aware of the injustices and suffering that poisoned the lives of the poor and the powerless. In Our Dynasty's Warning Bell of Poesy (Guochao shiduo) of 1859, Zhang Yingchang compiled an anthology of two thousand or so of their often startlingly poignant poems.[9] The themes covered include droughts, famines, flooding and drowning by high tides and swollen rivers; taxes, conscription, the exactions of local bullies and money-lenders; not to mention landlords demanding rent, backed by threats of local government force, as well as the sale of children and their parents' suicides due to poverty. They told of the back-breaking toil of women, both in textile manufacture and farming—for female work of this latter sort was becoming common in Qing times, in areas under the greatest demographic pressure of a denser population—and of the savage psychological mistreatment by some mothers-in-law of their daughters-in-law. In contrast, but with strong ideological implications, they also depicted the joys of devoted and uncomplaining married women, who rose above their difficulties to

---

[7] Li Ruzhen, Flowers in the Mirror, Berkeley 1965, ch. 90; henceforth FM.
[8] FM, ch. 16.
[9] Reprinted as the Qing Warning Bell of Poesy (Qing shiduo), 2 vols, Beijing 1960.

become loved and esteemed matriarchs at the end of their lives. These themes are accompanied by a miscellany of other topics: the pampered but submissive existence of girls raised and trained from birth to be sold as expensive secondary wives to the well-to-do; the precarious existence of travelling entertainers, tea-pickers, coal-miners and charcoal-burners, servants, soldiers and prisoners; and, most numerous of all, the seasonal labours and dreams, bitterness, frustrations and transient happinesses of farmers and their wives and children. These paintings in words form an unrolling scroll of otherwise unseen lives, with few if any parallels in other literatures. A warm and sympathetic human feeling runs through most of the poems, alongside open or implied condemnation for those exploiting others,[10] yet there is no awareness that a social, political or ideological *system* might be at least in part to blame for people's sufferings. Understanding that this was perhaps, even probably, the case had potentially revolutionary implications; but it was a change of perspective that began to occur in China only toward the end of the nineteenth century, mainly as the result of Western influences and, to some extent, of Western example.

Dangers of absurdity

By the start of the 1920s, however, there erupted what can only be called 'a crisis of absurdity' in the more developed parts of Chinese society. Timms, in his book on the Austrian satirist Karl Kraus at about the same time, has pointed to 'the contradictions between a given social structure and the forms of consciousness in which it [is] apprehended' as the mechanism which produces a sense that life is absurd.[11] This is not a trivial matter. To feel that one's existence is absurd is a dangerous emotion. It is one that probably contributed, through the need for its denial and suppression, to the rise of National Socialism in Vienna, and then Germany. Such a sense of absurdity is probably a symptom of a transitional phase in the breakdown of an old pattern of meanings, whose inappropriateness is becoming ever more apparent, even though it retains a grip on people's minds. A comparable form of mental

---

[10] Counterbalanced on rare occasions by an insistence that even the government and money-lenders had their own problems—such as suppressing rebels and surviving the loss of loans that were not repaid—which deserved to be taken into consideration.

[11] Edward Timms, *Karl Kraus, Apocalyptic Satirist: Culture and Catastrophe in Habsburg Vienna*, New Haven 1986, p. 10.

self-torture, though of course in a Chinese cultural mode, spread through educated China during the early Republic; it was one of the psychological causes that drove a number of often brilliant and idealistic activists and intellectuals to form the early Chinese Communist Party. There was an aching need for an understanding of what was going on, in the midst of confusion and humiliation; a hunger for certainty, for mastery and for hope; in the end, whatever the cost.

Many readers will want to argue that there were enough valid objective reasons for people to want to turn this way. This is not entirely untrue. A hard-headed, self-critical, non-dogmatic Marxist analysis based on facts could have been both useful and inspirational. But to say this is to miss the point. This was not what the founders of the Party wanted. Once they had acquired their quasi-religious doctrine and, in due course, the apologetics of a winding path through history—which let them tolerate the otherwise intolerable changes of Party line, as Ai Siqi was before long to preach in *The Philosophy of the Masses (Dazhong zhexue)*[12]—they bent their knowledge of reality to fit their beliefs, with ultimately terrible consequences. Many readers will understandably ask for some proof that such bending took place; as it happens, there are a few instances where this can be done directly from the CCP's own records. Let us therefore diverge from the main theme for a moment, and consider an example based on Hsiao Tso-liang's *The Land Revolution in China, 1930–1934*.[13]

Rural myths and realities

Landholding patterns varied from place to place in China, but, following John Buck's well-known survey of the late 1920s, it is fair to say that in broad terms the early-twentieth-century farming sector was a world of smallholders: over a half of farmers were owners, under one-third were part-owners, and 17 per cent were tenants. The median size of farm was a diminutive 1.34 hectares, and land was not in itself a very good investment for those with funds, other than for increased security, when

---

[12] I have not been able to find a copy of the original edition, but, so far as can be told, the theory was long-established by this time. The basic idea is that since the phenomena of the world are always changing, our ideas must change to correspond with this development. So, to put it crudely, different views become 'true' under different circumstances. See *Philosophy of the Masses*, p. 123.
[13] Hsiao Tso-liang, *The Land Revolution in China, 1930–1934: A Study of Documents*, Seattle 1969; for my review of it, see Mark Elvin, 'Early Communist Land Reform and the Kiangsi Rural Economy', *Modern Asian Studies*, vol. 4, no. 2, April 1970.

compared to usury and trade. A significant proportion of the larger land-lords tended to be city-dwelling absentees with scattered holdings, with a limited or nonexistent personal presence in local communities. Socio-economic divisions between peasants were for the most part slight, and those that existed were mostly compressed within narrow limits, while social mobility both up and down between these limits, or, for a few, even beyond them, was relatively rapid. When the CCP armed forces occupied part of Jiangxi province at the beginning of the 1930s, they had to draw the finest of fine distinctions between categories of peasants deemed to be ideologically distinct, in order to create even a semblance of the 'rural feudal power' spoken of by Mao. They had, for example, to use as a criterion the *percentage* of household income drawn from rents, which could easily brand a temporarily labour-poor household unfairly as an exploiter. In one county the first survey of land ownership found 1,576 'landlord' and 'rich peasant' households; Mao's supplementary investigation of 1933 then found 536 more; but a re-examination of cases resulted in 941 clearing themselves of these 'exploiting' statuses. Thus the Party ended after all this effort with only 74 per cent of the percent-age found by the initial survey.[14]

The yoyo-like revision of the figures speaks eloquently of the practical difficulty of creating a plausible picture of a stable, stratified class *struc-ture*, with data drawn from reality; for reality here predominantly took the form of a class *continuum*, with permanently unstable statuses. The speed of social mobility meant that the CCP investigators decided that 'landlord' or 'rich peasant' status could be regarded as having been estab-lished in three years. But even they wrestled to categorize cases such as that of a landless hired labourer who rose in twenty years to being a landlord and money-lender. One unusually plausible CCP document also observed that 'well-to-do middle peasants constitute a considerable proportion of the population in the rural districts [of Jiangxi province].'[15] When the general economic level is low, small differences can of course count for a lot; but it is a reasonable guess that the land reform move-ment drew most of its support by mobilizing the fierce competitiveness of those who felt they were losing out against those who were close to being their social equals, rather than from any structural antagonism between clearly differentiated classes. Such a class structure had indeed earlier existed in many parts of central and southern China; lasting until,

---

[14] Hsiao, *Land Revolution*, p. 117.   [15] Hsiao, *Land Revolution*, p. 263.

in the seventeenth century, it was largely demolished by tenant-serf uprisings.[16] It should not be forgotten that there have been important *premodern* revolutions in China, even if less extensive and dramatic than those resulting from contact with the modern West.

Shanghai satires

We return to our main theme, the crisis of absurdity, with *Tides in the Human Sea* (*Renhai chao*) by Ping Jinya, who wrote under the pseudonym of 'Mr. Spider in the Web'.[17] This five-volume book, first published in 1927, seems to have been a best-seller by the mid-1930s, and was probably more widely read then than the literature that we now think of as canonical for the Republican period. It is a picture, with interweaving plots, of the society of Shanghai and the countryside around it, starting in the years following the fall of the Manchus. The scenes are drawn with the keen and cynical eye of a lawyer, which was Ping's profession, and a merciless, grotesquely inventive humour whose realistic detail somehow persuades us that he is telling us something important of the truth. Life is surreal, aleatoric, riddled by stupidity and superstition, and driven by greed, lust and deception, with those who are sweet-natured, straightforward, and naïve as its victims. At fleeting moments Ping's underlying sadness at this state of affairs shows through the funny but somewhat heartless surface of his writing, as does his love for the beauty of the world of nature when compared with the mire of the human world; these two emotions give his satire a sudden and unexpected depth. Every historically revered conception and institution is treated either as false or else ill-founded and humanly damaging. Terms for 'Heaven' occur most

---

[16] See for instance the rebel serfs who called themselves the 'Levelling Kings' (*chanping wang*) of Jizhou in Jiangxi in 1644–45: 'Whenever they held a drinking bout they would order the masters to kneel and pour out the wine for them. They would slap them across the cheeks and say: "We are all of us equally men. What right had you to call us serfs? From now on it is going to be the other way around!"' See Fu Yiling, *Ming-Qing nongcun shehui jingji* [The society and economy of villages under the Ming and Qing], Beijing 1961, p. 109. Note, though, that quasi-servile status was geographically irregularly distributed in late Ming times, being important mainly in central and southern China, and far from existing everywhere.

[17] Ping Jinya, *Renhai Chao* (1927), Shanghai 1935; published by Zhongyang shudian. Henceforth THS. This work was republished in 1991 in simplified characters by the Shanghai *guji chubanshe*, with some useful background material. I would like to thank my former colleague, Professor Rudolf Wagner of the University of Heidelberg, for help in dating the first edition.

commonly in the speech of blatant liars or hypocrites. The effigy of a minor deity, a low-level City God (*chenghuang*), is the object of hilarious sexual mockery when a brothel madame from Shanghai stages the glamorous 'post-mortem' marriage of a lifelike wax model of her favourite and most profitable prostitute to the God, in order to stop the woman's legitimate husband from claiming her back. The husband is, like the local officials, bribed for playing his part in this charade, and he is solemnly given a fake coffin, which he then surreptitiously throws away in a ditch, to be spared the cost of a funeral.

Though simple people may often think the contrary, Ping insists the course of human events is not ruled by the justice of Buddhist-style moral cause and effect: people's lives are casually ruined by accident, often from the personal malice or bad temper of locally powerful bullies, sometimes based on a false understanding of actions and motives. Or, equally casually, they can be enriched. The traditional family is shown as institutionalized oppression and unhappiness. A woman will often do better emotionally and financially, Ping implies, by going off—with her daughter if need be—to work in a reputable brothel. In the cruellest case described, the traditionally honourable fidelity of a young widow who is abused by her late husband's family on the basis of malicious unfounded gossip, leading her to commit suicide, is presented as doubly horrible because it is *meaningless*, being motivated by outdated Confucian ideals in which it is impossible to believe any longer. Though sincere, the suicide is mocked by most bystanders, who assume it is just make-believe intended to put pressure on her father-in-law. The widow is also deluded in thinking that she will be reunited with her husband in the world beyond death, which, as traditionally imagined, is a fiction.

With their mischievous little tricks, senior members of local communities and arbitrators of disputes are almost universally presented as preaching morality and doing exactly the opposite in their quest for money; and as enjoying hurting those whom they dislike by the use of their petty powers. Younger Buddhist monks are shown as panting for sex and pornography, or addicted to drugs, and taking the first possible chance to rob their temples and run away. Traditional medicine and pharmacology appear as practices of conscious fraud under the pretence of learned medical sales-talk that is no more than nonsense in an intellectual sense, but at times literally lethal in its effects. Ping is artist enough to balance evil behaviour with a few examples of honesty and altruism. The last, though, is shown as having sometimes unavoidably to be done by intrinsically improper means, such as using inventive lies to secure forgiveness for someone wrongly accused.

Shanghai itself, though by the late 1920s already a high-speed engine of financial, commercial and modern industrial growth, is experienced by Ping as nothing but ingenious and remorseless exploitation, in which human life has been separated from nature and expresses itself for the most part through deceit, seductive fakery and grotesque self-parody. There is, for example, a sequence of adroitly convincing scenes show-ing the world of the city beggars as a simulacrum of the 'respectable' world, with its own social stratification, laws and government, bosses, territories, scholars, even the 'modernization' of begging techniques—and moral standards that are not in fact any worse. The now useless traditional learning of fifty years before is attacked by 'Dr. Duplex' (*Er xiansheng*), once a grade-one graduate of the former imperial exams, but now a sort of beggar who lives by telling fortunes and teaching the Chinese script to a few poor children:

> My only hatred is against my parents. Why did they have to make me study since my earliest youth? Why did they have to teach me to recognize written characters? Why did they want me to take the examinations and advance in my studies, so inflicting on me this sort of misery?
>
> If instead, from my earliest days, they had sent me to a house of pleasure to learn how to boil water, or to a rickshaw company to learn how to pull a rickshaw, I would have been content from then till now, and in no way obliged to suffer for these many years.[18]

Duplex adds that when he dies and goes to the underworld, he intends to settle accounts with his father. So much for filial piety.

In *Tides in the Human Sea*, traditional Chinese literary culture has become an unpleasant mixture of half-remembered classics and ill-digested Western ideas like those of the Realist School (*xieshipai*), which *littéra-teurs* use as a handy way of glorifying third-rate poems about such things as mosquitoes and lice in a scholar's bedroom.[19] Writers have to earn their living by writing gossip for cheap newspapers and copy for adver-tisements, while fantasizing (stupidly) about their own tragic greatness.[20]

---

[18] THS, II, p. 118.   [19] THS, II, p. 36.
[20] See Mark Elvin, 'Littérateurs and Voyeurs: Shanghai Men of Letters of the 1930s', in Rachel May and John Minford, eds, *A Birthday Book for Brother Stone: For David Hawkes, at Eighty*, Hong Kong 1999.

Ping, it should be added, regards almost everything distinctively Western as pretentious, oversold, and more often than not harmful. Thus newspapers titillate their readers rather than giving useful news: in one episode a young wife, the well-intentioned, would-be modernizing head of a primary school, is reading a heart-breaking newspaper story about a Pekinese dog that has been crushed by a car in Shanghai; her husband observes that the vast floods outside which, unnoticed by her, have swept away their school and forced many peasants to flee, are not even mentioned in its pages.

Magical Maoism

There had to be medicine for this spiritual anomie; and such medicine could also easily serve as a powerful means of political mobilization. It is thus understandable that the Chinese Communists, besides attempting more practical measures, some sensible and some not, further provided the Chinese people with an alternative story in which to live. To see what resulted in its clearest form, it is simplest to take an example from near the end of the period of what might be called 'ideologically alive Maoism', *The Children of the Western Sands (Xisha Ernü)* by Hao Ran, published in 1974 in a first run of a million copies.[21] The two-volume novel is set on islands in the South China Sea, historically disputed by several governments. The first volume covers the war with Japan; the second, the years after 1949 and the building of socialism on the islands. The book is written in a brilliant and lucid style, and many of its ideals are—in the abstract—altruistic and worthy, even noble, ones. Its most serious fault, though, apart from a chauvinism that obliterates all other moral concerns (not a problem unique to the Chinese), is that it portrays Maoist morality as having an essentially magical quality, which is a self-deception with cruel consequences. The saddest aspect of its historical role, however, is that it was peddled by power-holders, mostly for short-term political purposes, who had no belief whatever that its messages applied to their own actions.

The story is that of Abao, 'Jewel', who survives her dangerous birth on a fishing-boat during a storm due—it is implied—to her father Cheng Liang's impassioned ideological plea to the elements of the skies and seas to let the dawn return to the poor and downtrodden, and for girls

---

[21] Hao Ran, *Xisha Ernü*, Beijing 1974. 2 vols: I. *Healthy Tendencies (Zhengqi pian)*, II. *Lofty Ambitions (Qizhi pian)*. Henceforth cws.

to be valued at their true worth again. Soon afterwards, her fearless mother dies resisting the efforts of the local Fishing Boss, a collaborator of the Japanese, to force her to act as a wet-nurse for a Japanese military crony, and sinks 'with her heart at ease to the depths of the seas of the Ancestral Land, becoming one with its rocks and shoals'.[22] This theme of geo-spiritual absorption is an old solution, but in a new formulation—both patriotic and free from superstition—to the question of what happens to people after death.

Before long Abao's father learns from the Communist underground movement of 'the Great Star of Salvation of the poor people of the whole country—Chairman Mao', and when he is admitted to the Party 'for the first time he really and truly knew that his life had a meaning'.[23] A single father, he has his daughter brought up by all his guerrilla comrades together, and conditions her to an indomitable endurance that leaves even the hardened soldiers in awe. When, after the Revolution, Cheng Liang has to arrange emergency supplies in a battle against the South Vietnamese, he puts his daughter last on the list, knowing that she will hold out when no one else can. The effects of this can also be seen in her attitude to sexual stirrings as she matures. Physical proximity to comrades of the other sex is no longer seen as morally dangerous, due to the strength of the new generation's inner psychological controls.

For Cheng Liang, developing the Western Sands is an inspiring activity, but not everyone is happy in the new two-class society of cadres who direct, and people who obey. Almost every family tries to get their children out of the commune and into Canton, for special training and a career. Abao, who has been sent to college, quits early on the grounds that all the people going there have the wrong motives, merely wanting a personal career, and 'would do anything to avoid returning to a fishing village to catch fish'. Her father supports her against fierce criticism, saying: 'You are much more advanced than we are! Your father must learn well from you, you of the new generation! . . . *Among comrades there can be no old and no young*'.[24] Thus the oldest Chinese principle of all, the superior authority of age, was rejected.

When a traitor spying for the South Vietnamese makes a covert night-time getaway in a small boat, Abao swims after him, holding a rifle above

---

[22] CWS, I, p. 35.   [23] CWS, I, pp. 65, 75.   [24] CWS, II, pp. 38, 41.

her head, and then—in a symbolic reversal of her mother's death—rises from the sea, boards the boat and kills him.

> She pressed her young face, her slightly flushed face, lovingly against the chamber of the rifle that was grasped in her hand.
> The chamber of the rifle was warm too.
> The waves leapt happily at her side. Was it because they wished to come on board the sampan to hug her, or to hold her hand affectionately?[25]

Hao Ran makes justified killing seem beautiful, and nature a willing accomplice.

The book culminates by exalting the magic of moral power. First, Cheng Liang dismisses mere economics in planning, declaring for instance that a new boat costs 'only sweat'. It is also dangerous, he says, to become dependent on specialists for such things as engines: people must be able to do all these technical things for themselves. This is not altogether ill-judged. But later, much more dramatically, the unarmed islanders in a fishing boat are presented as staring down South Vietnamese naval power by sheer bravado and willpower, threatening the irresistible revenge of China if they are harmed. Then, when the conflict grows more serious, Abao's husband, Sea Dragon (*Hailong*), a captain in the Chinese Navy, prevails in a desperate battle against the South Vietnamese, even though they have disabled his ship's steering gear. He does this by following his chief helmsman's suggestion that the crew form a group to shift the wheel with their bare hands, even though this means standing up to their chests in blood-stained sea-water, while others form a human chain to relay his steering directions down from the bridge. The glory of the revolutionary human being is to become the ultimate interchangeable part, both superior and subordinate to the machine that he or she serves.

Crumbling prestige

A decade later, once Deng Xiaoping's reforms were well under way, this story and its dreams were forgotten as if they had never existed. Indeed, they were increasingly made fun of. It would be unwise, though, to assume that the prevailing story will not change again. How and why did such immense changes happen so rapidly between the worlds of the first two works—*Flowers in the Mirror* and the *Warning Bell of Qing Poesy*—

---

[25] CWS, II, pp. 181–2.

and those of the second two—*Tides in the Human Sea* and *Children of the Western Sands?* The core of the answer is that the late-imperial Chinese polity, compared to most others, was to an exceptional degree a *prestige structure*. Why this was crucial needs a little explaining.[26] A prestige structure depends on the creation and maintenance of an image that inspires respect and fear in those who are in contact with it. In addition it must present itself as the guarantor of a future that is thereby destined to arrive; those involved must be associated with it if they are to enjoy good fortune. Prestige of this sort is an all-or-none reputation: a regime—or an ideology—either has it or it does not.

The ancient concept of the 'Mandate of Heaven' (*Tianming*) expressed an idea typical of a prestige structure: a dynasty was seen as possessing or as having lost the Mandate, depending on whether or not it had secured the hearts and minds of the people. In modern times, an implicit and more complex secular version seems to have replaced this. A government and a society are seen to have, or to have lost, what might be called the 'Mandate of History'. There is no standard and commonly understood term in the Chinese language for this idea, though it is not hard to paraphrase. To an increasing number of scholars and thinkers, looking back from the second half of the nineteenth century, China's relative world-historical success prior to the late eighteenth century seemed to suggest that the Qing state, like its predecessors, had once had a claim to this mandate, but had lost it in the course of the nineteenth century when the Chinese empire and its knowledge appeared weak and backward, when compared with the modern West. And the question also began to be raised: was this failure due not just to a particular government but also to China's traditional beliefs and values?

Prestige structures are relatively rigid. Perceived overt change risks suggesting past error, and this damages the image. So long as the image is preserved, however, such structures can have considerable flexibility in secret. Once the image begins to deteriorate, a process of positive feedback can accelerate, and lead to sudden collapse. A bandwagon mentality develops: most people resist changing allegiances at first, but once they think they can detect a decisive shift they will move quickly to associate themselves with it. This helps to explain both the swift spread

---

[26] For an earlier discussion of these themes, see Mark Elvin, 'How Did the Cracks Open? Origins of the Subversion of China's Late-Traditional Culture by the West', *Thesis Eleven*, no. 57, May 1999.

of enthusiasm for new movements in China, and the abruptness of disillusionment with them. For politicians in a prestige system, maintaining the façade is the key to survival. They resist even the smallest concession since there is no knowing when the catastrophe of positive feedback may trigger collapse. Control over mental attitudes is vital; the exposure of aspects of reality that cast doubt on the façade is not just seen as embarrassing, but—in a way correctly—as dangerous. This is usually complemented, but not counterbalanced, by cynicism among intelligent people, who possess a certain understanding of the logic of this sort of system, about what is really going on behind the scenes. It was due to a political condition of this kind that the forcible establishment of a handful of Western diplomats in Beijing in the 1850s at first provoked such panic-stricken xenophobia among many of the top Chinese officials.

At approximately the same time as this was happening, a remarkable rebellion called the Heavenly Kingdom of Great Peace occupied much of the Yangzi valley and almost overthrew the Manchu-Qing dynasty. If it had been supported by the foreign powers, rather than resisted, it is very likely that it would have done so. Its ideology, the new story in which it tried to make its followers live, was based on borrowings from a Christian missionary tract blended with elements of both conventional and Utopian Confucianism. It tried to smash popular religion, Daoism and Buddhism as superstitions, and was driven by a vision of what was, in broad terms, a collective economic future. It mounted a crusade against extra-marital sex, opium and gambling. It bred a sense of guilt in its followers, and a desire for repentance and redemption. In other words it used and developed most of the psycho-social potentialities that were later to be exploited by Chinese Communism. Nature was seen as a manifestation of God's unified power, not the workings of spirits and deities. Humankind was a single family, all people being God's children. An innovation in the Chinese context was the Taiping claim that Evil came from a single source, the Devil, identified with the ruler of the Buddhist purgatories, instead of being a multitude of separate afflictions, rather like moral diseases. The idealized Taiping economic system was never put into practice. But the social liberation of women was made a reality to a great extent, including the recruitment of female soldiers. The writings of the founder's cousin, Hong Ren'gan showed that a synthesis of elements of Christian doctrine with elements of Confucianism was quite possible—he defined God, for example, as the self-creating and self-ending power that gave form to forms throughout the universe, which made him not unlike the Dao. Hong also promulgated a programme for technical modernization, and the elements of a welfare state.

Silent revolution

The Heavenly Kingdom was strategically defeated in 1864, ultimately as a result of the internal quarrels of its increasingly corrupt leadership. Numerous lesser but still serious rebellions were crushed, including the reconquest of the recently acquired, but then lost, Eastern Turkestan. After this there followed more than thirty years of political life in a straitjacket of conservatism, as senior politicians were fearful of the risks of almost any changes other than necessary tactical adaptations to foreign pressures. A start was made on railroad building and on telegraph lines; modern industry grew fast in Shanghai and one or two other cities; some military officers were trained abroad, and a navy was created. But little more than that. Paradoxically, though, it was during this time, especially the 1890s, that the ideas which sustained the inherited imperial order were undermined, almost imperceptibly, by the persistent questioning of a small number of concerned officials and the growing anxieties of a few remarkable members of the scholar class.

If there was one *deep* Chinese political 'revolution' of modern times, it has to be—weirdly but undeniably—what went on in these seemingly almost silent decades. Why? Because at their end, scriptural Confucianism was strategically dead. 'Dead' in the sense that there were no more creative thinkers of any importance who were able to revitalize and develop it.[27] And, equally critically, the outlines of new policies had been formulated, even if their difficulties were not yet fully understood. The early sprouts of local and then, briefly, higher-level democratic institutions in the first decade of the twentieth century,[28] and then the revolution of 1911, are well-known evidence of the seriousness of the impact of conceptual

---

[27] See Mark Elvin, 'The Collapse of Scriptural Confucianism', in *Papers on Far Eastern History* 41, March 1990.
[28] On the earliest phase, the only full account remains Mark Elvin, 'The Gentry Democracy in Shanghai, 1905–1914', PhD thesis, University of Cambridge 1967. See also chapters 5 and 6 on Shanghai in Elvin, *Another History: Essays on China from a European Perspective*, Broadway, NSW 1996. For the later developments, see John Fincher, *Chinese Democracy, the Self-Government Movement in Local, Provincial and National Politics, 1905–1914*, London 1981, and Mireille Delmas-Marty and Pierre-Etienne Will, eds, *La Chine et la démocratie*, Paris 2007.

change, even though they did not live up to their earlier promise. But the Chinese government is also, in a sense, following even *today*, as a major aspect of its foreign strategy, a refined and more sophisticated version of that first proposed by perhaps the most important of these questioners of existing orthodoxy, Zheng Guanying. Zheng was the originator of the concept of 'commercial warfare' (*shang zhan*) as a way of defeating the Westerners with their own weapons.[29]

The scholars who wrote on current affairs in these years almost all agreed that something was seriously wrong with their country, by comparison with others which seemed to be prospering. Interwoven with more transient concerns, six themes with long-term implications dominated their debates. The first concerned the interpretation of history: was the present era just another chapter in the long saga of conflicts between the Chinese and the 'barbarians', or was the age a qualitatively new one? If so, in what respects? Was some cooperation, rather than outright conflict, both possible and desirable? The second theme focused on sovereignty: how could China best resist the military and commercial threats from the West? Would something on which everyone agreed, namely the reinvigoration of 'the resolve of the masses' (*zhongzhi*)—the phrase used by Liu Xihong—suffice, if combined with strengthened traditional military technology? Or should modern weapons be acquired, either by manufacture or purchase?[30] Should China imitate, with its own colonialism, imperialism and religious propaganda, the recent settlement of Western peoples in lands other than their own ('colonialism' in the strict traditional sense of the word), or the Western conquest of other people's lands ('imperialism' in the traditional sense of the word), or the Western sending abroad of merchants to sell their goods, and of preachers to convert foreigners to their faith—in other words, should China support the efforts of Confucian missionaries?

Thirdly, vital cultural questions were at stake. If China decided it was obliged for safety's sake to adopt a selection of Western cultural features, would this not, as Wang Tao asked, 'virtually amount to making China

---

[29] Often unfactual and rhetorical on this topic, but with a marksman's eye for the vital spots. See his *Shengshi weiyan* (Words of Warning to a Prosperous Age) in Jian Bocan et al., eds, *Wuxu bianfa* (The Reforms of 1898), Shanghai 1957, I, pp. 83–7.
[30] Zhongguo shixuehui, ed., *Yangwu yundong* [The Foreign Affairs Movement], Shanghai 1962, vol. I, p. 284. Henceforth YWYD I. Apart from items at the end on Zheng Guanying, all the documentation for the section that follows is drawn from this volume, pp. 263–599.

into a nation of Westerners?'[31] So how should the cultural identity of the Chinese be preserved—by intensified indoctrination, or by preserving the emphasis on sensitive concern for others (*ren*) and a sense of public spirit (*yi*) which, Wang believed, had spared China the abrupt rise and collapse of other civilizations, based on force alone? A fourth theme was economic: should Western machinery be used to replace human labour, and to increase output? If so, what were the likely effects on moral values of creating a society unreasonably attracted to profits; and on employment, since machines would take away some people's jobs; and also on natural resources, especially if the latter were exhausted by the increased demands placed on them? Even Xue Fucheng, a passionate admirer of the Western technological breakthrough, and its basis in experiment, noted that 'there is a limit at which the growth of every living thing stops.'[32] Wang Bing however argued in opposition, but with some justification for this period, that many of the techniques of Chinese labour-intensive farming were too delicate ever to be mechanized, apart from pumping water, and that ordinary peasants could never afford machines.[33]

The fifth theme involved political questions. Since it was believed by almost all officials and scholars that a major source of the strength of Western countries was the close relationship and mutual understanding between their governments and their peoples, would it be useful to China to introduce at least some degree of democracy? If so, how much and of what kind? Finally, the sixth theme to be addressed was the question of science: appreciation for Western advances in this field came late, but, asked Zheng Guanying, was it not the most vital aspect of all recent Western creations?

> The reason that *gezhi* {experimental science} exhausts the [secrets of the] springs of Heaven and Earth, and explains the Primal Principles of the Ten Thousand Things, is to supplement the workings of Heaven {sc. natural processes} with human actions, and to put the workings of Heaven {sc. nature} into the service of human affairs. When these pattern-principles {sc. laws of nature} are understood, it is possible for one person to provide for a thousand or ten thousand or a million. Can our China, with her population of four hundred million, and holding the first place on the five continents, [go on] treating her masses as if they were children, and not, as a matter of urgency, make plans for 'nourishing them by instruction'?[34]

---

[31] YWYD I, p. 512.   [32] YWYD I, p. 391.   [33] YWYD I, pp. 460–1.
[34] *Wuxu bianfa*, I, p. 74.

In other words, Zheng was proposing general education in the natural sciences. Moving beyond the practical matters, which he put first, he further imagined that in the course of time, Chinese pattern-principles (*li*) and the numbers (*shu*) of Western science might be harmoniously combined to discover 'the central axis of human nature and destiny' (*xingming zhi shuniu*).[35] Even allowing for some partial links with earlier Ming/Qing period thinkers, especially those like Fang Yizhi who had for a time had links with the Jesuits in the seventeenth century, and a cultural nostalgia for *li*, this was a radical change of vision.

This debate did not of course end in a single agreed programme; but it did identify a set of problems for China, relating to what we loosely call political, economic and social 'modernity', which permanently altered the underlying nature of policy debate in China. It is also possible to argue that, in more sophisticated forms, it was not only the major intellectual factor in extinguishing scriptural Confucianism, but that, in many implicit forms, it has also outlasted scriptural Maoism. There were heavyweight accidental factors in both of China's formally recognized political revolutions: for that of 1911 it was the extraordinary ineptitude of the remaining Qing politicians, who could easily have come to an arrangement with the gentry- and official-class leaders of the movement for a constitution; for that of 1949 it was the escape of the CCP from the closing grip of the Nationalists in the middle 1930s, deflected by the attempted conquest of China by the Japanese. The radical conceptual and cultural realignment associated with the 1870s, 1880s and 1890s has, in contrast, much more of the character of something that was all but inevitable and irreversible. At least, it is interesting to consider such a point of view.

---

[35] *Wuxu bianfa*, 1, p. 44.

ANDY MERRIFIELD

CROWD POLITICS

Or, 'Here Comes Everybuddy'

I N JAMES JOYCE's dazzlingly inventive *Finnegans Wake*, the hero is a certain Humphrey Chimpden Earwicker, HCE for short, whose dreaming mind becomes the psychological space of the *Wake*'s drama. If *Ulysses*'s Leopold Bloom is everyday man, then Earwicker, or HCE, is every*night* man. Thus the epithet Joyce gives him in Chapter 2: 'Here Comes Everybody'. The initials HCE were the 'normative letters', Joyce said, of a universal dreaming figure; a sort of Jungian archetypal image of our collective, desiring unconscious, reliving in a single night's sleep the whole of human history. 'An imposing everybody he always indeed looked,' Joyce joked of Earwicker, 'constantly the same as and equal to himself and magnificently well worthy of any and all such universalization.'[1]

For a while I dreamed of writing a book with the title, *Here Comes Everybody*. An urban book, because today urban life is, famously, the social environment to which everybody is coming. Only a few decades ago, a majority of the world's population lived in the countryside; today, most people live in cities, and soon that majority is set to become almost everybody; billions of people, inhabiting a vast global *banlieue*. In 2008 Clay Shirky, a communications professor at New York University, beat me to it, publishing a book called *Here Comes Everybody* with the intriguing subtitle: 'The Power of Organizing without Organizations'. I gravitated toward it, in expectation of high-spirited Joycean puns and artistry; but there were none to be had. *Here Comes Everybody* is an artless book, un-Joycean in its lack of existential depth. Yet perhaps lack of content is the point, in Shirky's account of the new forms of sociability engendered by a digital age; a world where everybody is getting together on Facebook and Twitter.

Here Comes Everybody quickly became a best-selling bible for the new social media movement, with a thesis that could apply as much to the corporate sector as to grassroots activism. In this latter respect, it was not far removed from John Holloway's 'change the world without taking power'—organize without organizations. Shirky's appeal was his inclusive 'everybody': social media had the power to de-professionalize select sectors, like journalism, and create collaborative work for 'ordinary' non-specialist people. Groups could now operate 'with a birthday party's informality and a multi-national's scope'.[2] This line came under attack from Malcolm Gladwell in the *New Yorker*, who argued that online activism inspired only 'weak-tie' radicalism. It could not provide what social change really needs: people risking life and limb, as in the 1960s sit-ins that kick-started the black civil-rights movement. What mattered was the physicality of bodies being present in space; the 'strong-tie' connections that bonded people to a cause and to each other: 'The kind of activism associated with social media isn't like this at all. Twitter is a way of following people you may have never met. Facebook is a tool for efficiently managing your acquaintances.' They had their advantages, but 'weak ties seldom lead to high-risk activism'—'we're a long way from the lunch counters of Greensboro.'[3]

Lost cities

Arguably Shirky and Gladwell are both right and both wrong; each thesis is insufficient in itself. Is it not possible to conceive of activism today as at once weak-tie and high-risk, both online and offline at the same time? And if so, would the 'strong-tie' space in which an offline 'Here Comes

---

[1] James Joyce, *Finnegans Wake*, New York 1976, p. 32. When Joyce lived in Zurich, he and Jung got together a few times; Jung was convinced that Joyce was schizophrenic. Always a sceptic of psychoanalysis, Joyce himself refused to let the Swiss psychologist psychoanalyse him. Later on, desperate about his daughter Lucia's mental condition, he relented and agreed to allow Jung to analyse her. The sessions, however, proved disastrous and Joyce soon broke off contact with Jung. In several sections of *Finnegans Wake*, the psychologist is satirized: '*Jungfraud*'; instead of *jungfrau* (the German for young woman), Joyce puns both Jung and Freud: he saw them equally as 'frauds'.
[2] Clay Shirky, *Here Comes Everybody*, New York 2008, p. 48.
[3] Malcolm Gladwell, 'Small Change', *New Yorker*, 4 October 2010.

Everybody' expresses itself necessarily be urban? In the 1960s, when the majority of people on Earth were still rural dwellers, the 'right to the city' was theorized as a radical 'cry and demand' by the French urbanist and philosopher, Henri Lefebvre. Fifty years on, now that Lefebvre's urban revolution has largely consummated itself, how does the 'right to the city' fare? For Lefebvre, the political utility of a concept did not lie in its tallying with reality, but in enabling us to glimpse a 'virtual reality', as he often called it; one that is waiting to be born. In one of his final texts, he lamented the end of the traditional city: nobody today could write as gaily and lyrically about city life as Apollinaire had once written about Paris. The more the city had grown and spread its tentacles, the more degraded had social relations become. For Lefebvre, the 'menace' was that this amorphous monster would become a planetary metamorphosis, totally out of control.[4]

As hitherto rural worlds had been urbanized, traditional forms of work—secure, decent-paying jobs—seemed to melt into air. Once, people had migrated to the city looking for steady factory jobs; but those industries had gone belly-up or cleared out to somewhere cheaper; cities had lost their manufacturing bases, their 'popular' productive centres. Millions of peasants and smallholders, thrown off their land by agribusiness or the dynamics of the world market, came to an alien habitat that was now neither meaningfully urban nor rural; the result of a vicious process of dispossession, sucking people into the city while spitting others out of the gentrifying centre, forcing poor urban old-timers and vulnerable newcomers onto an expanding periphery. The outcome as Lefebvre described it was a paradoxical dialectic, in which 'centres and peripheries oppose one another'. But the demarcation between these two worlds was not defined by any simple urban-rural or North–South divide. Centres and peripheries were immanent within the 'secondary circuits' of capital itself. If ground rents and property prices offered better rates of return than other industrial sectors, capital—spearheaded by banks, financial institutions, big property companies and realtors—would slosh into portfolios of property speculation. Profitable locations would be deluged, as secondary-circuit flows became torrential, while other zones would be desiccated through disinvestment. The centre thus created its own periphery, the two existing side-by-side, cordoned off from one other, everywhere.

---

4 Henri Lefebvre, 'Quand la ville se perd dans une métamorphose planétaire', *Le Monde diplomatique*, May 1989.

The giant industrial city that Friedrich Engels had documented was being destroyed by its own progeny. Industrialization had bequeathed something new: planetary urbanization. Rural regions had become absorbed into post-industrial production and financial speculation, swallowed up by an 'urban fabric', ceaselessly corroding the residue of agrarian life. At the same time, the notion of citizen and that of city-dweller had been wrenched apart. Cities' inhabitants now experienced a tragic form of proximity without sociability. Lefebvre's tonality throughout the essay is Céline-like in its journey to the end of the night; yet he could not resist a few Whitmanesque flourishes, throwing out one final thought about what a new democratic vista might look like. The 'right to the city', he concluded, now implied 'nothing less than a new revolutionary conception of citizenship', in which city-dweller and citizen would somehow embrace one another again.

But, as ever with Lefebvre, the proposition raised as many questions as it answered. Right to *what* city? If urbanization is planetary, if the urban—or urban society—is everywhere, does this mean the right to the metropolitan region, the whole urban agglomeration, or just the right to the city's downtown? And if power is now global, does that not render Lefebvre's singular demand hopelessly archaic? Does it still make sense to talk about right to *the* city, as if this was something mono-centric and clear-cut? Moreover, is there any political purchase in defining citizenship through something 'urban', when urban territoriality itself has become so formless, so global in its reach? At the same time, never before has the urban process been so bound up with finance capital and with the caprices of the world's financial markets. The crucial term here is David Harvey's 'accumulation by dispossession', mobilizing Marx's theory of 'primitive accumulation' in a 21st-century neoliberal context. In *Capital*, Marx described primitive accumulation as the process of 'divorcing the producer from the means of production'—'when great masses of men are suddenly and forcibly torn from their means of subsistence, and hurled onto the labour-market as free, unprotected and rightless proletarians. The expropriation of the agricultural producer, of the peasant, from the soil is the basis of the whole process.'[5]

In advanced capitalism, Harvey argues, accumulation by dispossession marks out other terrain for speculation and market expansion:

---

[5] Karl Marx, *Capital*, vol. 1, London 1976, pp. 874–6.

asset-stripping through mergers and acquisitions, raiding of pension funds, biopiracy, privatization of hitherto common assets and the general pillaging of hitherto publicly-owned property. Under Haussmann's direction, the built urban form of 19th-century Paris became, simultaneously, a property machine and a means to divide and rule; today, neo-Haussmannization, integrating financial, corporate and state interests, sequesters land through forcible slum clearance and eminent domain, valorizing it while banishing former residents to the post-industrial hinterlands. In Harvey's formulation, the 'right to the city' has to be reconceived as global, because urbanization is now masterminded by transnational finance capital; on the other hand, the city itself still holds the key: the revolution 'has to be urban or nothing at all'.[6]

Yet even if we accept the 'urban' as a specific terrain for political struggle, what would the 'right to the city' actually look like? Would it resemble the Paris Commune, a great festival of merriment, people storming into the centre of town (when there was still a centre), occupying it, tearing down statues, abolishing rents for a while? If so, how would this deal with the problem Marx identified—those flows of capital and commodities? Even if people re-appropriated the downtown HQs of the big corporate and financial institutions, would this really destabilize 'the system'? In 20th-century revolutionary traditions, wresting control over urban areas has often been the final icing on the cake: by then, the social movement had already been built, the bonds already forged; taking control of the city announced the culmination of victory, the storming of the Winter Palace, the social movement's final, joyous fling. Often, revolutionary currents have flowed from the countryside onto the urban streets. In *Revolution in the Revolution*, Régis Debray described the city as the 'empty head', deaf to the plight of those who feel accumulation by dispossession the most; the rural hinterlands, mountain jungles, and abandoned *banlieues* provide the 'armed fist' of rebellion: 'The city, for the guerrilla movement, was a symbol, *the purpose of which was to create the conditions for a coup d'état in the capital*.'[7] Mao, Che, Castro, Ortega and Subcomandante Marcos would doubtless concur: the city does not so much radicalize as neutralize popular elements.

The city, from this standpoint, is not so much a Lefebvrian dialectical *oeuvre* as a Sartrean practico-inert, the prison-house of past actions that

[6] David Harvey, 'The Right to the City', NLR 53, Sept–Oct 2008.
[7] Régis Debray, *Revolution in the Revolution*, New York 1967, pp.76–7.

inhibit active praxis. The practico-inert announces that dead labour dominates over living labour, that praxis has been absorbed into the form of the city itself. It would explain the relative conformity of the world's urban populations today: unemployed, sub-employed and multi-employed attendants, cut off from the past yet somehow excluded from the future; deadened by the daily grind of hustling a living. This is a generation of urban dwellers for whom 'the right to the city' serves no purpose—either as a working concept or as a political programme. It remains at too high a level of abstraction to be existentially meaningful in everyday life. Put a little differently: the right to the city politicizes something that is too vast and at the same time too narrow to mobilize contemporary city-dwellers to act as a collectivity, a fused group. None of this is to deny the role of people fighting to maintain affordable rents or to ensure public spaces stay open. But to bundle these multiple struggles together under the loose rubric 'right to the city' is to render what is tellingly concrete somehow vacuously abstract. It is too vast, because the scale of the city is out of reach for most people living at street level; yet it is too narrow as well, because when people do protest and take to the streets *en masse*, they frequently reach out beyond the scale of the city. What is required is something closer to home—something one can touch and smell and feel—*and* something larger than life, something world-historical: a praxis that can somehow conjoin both realms at once.

Politics of the encounter

If the 'right to the city' is not working, perhaps the notion of the 'encounter' may be more useful in a political landscape in which new social media can become subversive weaponry. In a normative sense, the politics of the encounter can mediate between the lived and the historical; it can overcome the inertia of apparent mass and individual powerlessness. *Active* affects somehow replace *passive* affects; people start to recognize a 'singular essence', especially humiliated and exploited people, who encounter one another not always directly, but through a mode of relating to the world, through unstated forms of solidarity. As people find one another, they start to piece together common notions: they universalize, make more coherent what seems, on the face of it, only specific, lived experience. What appears particular is in fact general; our plight is that of many people. A politics of the encounter utters no rights, voices no claims. It just acts, affirms, takes back. An example of this in the United States would be Take Back the Land. Beginning in Miami in 2006, Take

Back the Land has borrowed its organizing and mobilizing techniques from Latin American social movements, particularly Brazil's Landless Workers' Movement (MST), with direct-action occupations of land and vacant lots, claiming and reclaiming abandoned and foreclosed properties for ordinary people, with the slogan 'Occupy, Resist, Produce'.

The recent upheavals in Tunisia, Egypt, Greece and Spain could be read as a dramatic politics of the encounter. In each case, whether in Tunis, Cairo, Athens, Madrid—or Manhattan, with the latest Occupy Wall Street protests—encounters unfolded in the heart of the city, yet the stake was not about the city *per se*; rather, it was about democracy, in conditions of capitalist crisis. A lot of the activism and organizing was done de-territorially—post-urban, if you will—through Facebook and Twitter; people experienced the encounter in terms of an affinity. One of the slogans raised by young Spaniards mobilizing across their recession-ravaged land was: 'no jobs, no houses, no pension, no fear.' Many in Spain were new protesters, with little to lose and everything to gain; disgusted with unions, who do nothing to represent their interests, and disillusioned with both PSOE and the PP. Protests bloomed over Twitter and Facebook, triggered by WikiLeaks documents exposing government officials' behaviour; the government's attempt to shut down previously legal websites through antipiracy laws riled this new social media generation. 'They were the spark,' one young protester claimed, like Mohamed Bouazizi's setting himself ablaze in Tunisia.[8]

In such encounters, it is the Joycean 'here comes everybody', rather than the 'right to the city', that is at stake. Affinity becomes the cement that bonds, perhaps only for a moment, but a moment that lingers, a lasting encounter, of people across frontiers and barriers. In the 1970s Murray Bookchin's *Post-Scarcity Anarchism* argued that the 'affinity group' could be regarded as 'a new type of extended family, in which kinship ties are replaced by deeply empathetic human relationships—relationships nourished by common revolutionary ideas and practice.'[9] In the context of an affinity-group encounter, 'class' perhaps evokes something meaningful principally in terms of a class-conscious ruling elite. The rest of us, those who do not rule, are an assorted and fragmented layering of

---

[8] *New York Times*, 7 June 2011.
[9] Murray Bookchin, *Post-Scarcity Anarchism*, London 1974, p. 221.

disparate people who are neither conscious of class nor motivated to act in its name. Still, these people, which is to say 'us', are often motivated by a desire to act against a ruling class, and against an undemocratic system that this class so evidently maintains. We who encounter one another, who find affinity with one another, are not so much class-conscious as collectively-conscious of an enemy; conscious of a desire to do something about that enemy, of wanting no truck with that enemy's game.

This takes a somewhat different tack to Marx and Engels in the *Communist Manifesto*, which spoke of the 'modern working class'. As Marshall Berman points out in a new preface to that famous tract, this layer has always been 'afflicted with a case of mistaken identity'.

> Many of Marx's readers have always thought that 'working class' meant only men in boots—in factories, in industry, with blue collars, with calloused hands, lean and hungry. These readers then note the changing nature of the workforce: increasingly white-collar, working in human services . . . and they infer the Death of the Subject, and conclude that the working class is disappearing and all hopes for it are doomed. Marx did not think the working class was shrinking: in all industrial countries it was already, or in the process of becoming, 'the immense majority'.

The basis for Marx's political arithmetic was rather simple. The modern working class is 'a class of labourers who live only so long as they find work, and who find work only so long as their labour increases capital. These workers, who must sell themselves piecemeal, are commodities, like every other article of commerce, and are constantly exposed to all the vicissitudes of competition and the fluctuations of the market.' The crucial factor is not working in a factory, or with your hands; nor is it necessarily anything to do with being poor. Rather, as Berman writes it is the need 'to sell your labour in order to live'—'to look at yourself in the mirror and think, "Now what have I got that I can sell?" '[10]

One virtue of this definition of the working class is its inclusiveness, its flexibility. By this reckoning, it would seem that the working class is practically 'here comes everybody'. It is a definition that hinges on a relationship to the means of production and to the global system of capital accumulation. But what seems a great conceptual virtue is also its major drawback, its potential failing. If the working class is now pretty much everywhere and everybody, then, like the city itself, it is at the same time

---

[10] Marshall Berman, 'Tearing Away Veils: *The Communist Manifesto*', in Karl Marx and Friedrich Engels, *The Communist Manifesto*, New York 2011.

pretty much nowhere, too; its definition serves no analytical or political function anymore. It no longer has any identifiable specificity as an object yearning to be a subject. In other words, the concept serves no strategic purpose, has no organizing pull. We may just as well label the working class 'the multitude', 'the general intellect', 'the people', or even 'Here Comes Everybody'. Maybe the working class is now a kind of *lumpen-concept*, setting itself free from its object like Marx's industrial reserve army: it is too flabby a notion to reveal anything meaningful to us, other than that we all need to find work to live. This is hardly news.

What is equally evident for millions of the world's population, is that they will never find work—and they know it. Instead they must find the means to bend the rules, to work the system for themselves. Others actively disaffiliate themselves from any labouring public, creating another life-form for themselves and their families and entering the ever-swelling ranks of a constituency that André Gorz provocatively termed a 'non-class'. The latent political muscle Marx accorded to the working class has not disappeared:

> Instead, it has been displaced and has acquired a more radical form in a new social area . . . It has the added advantage over Marx's working class of being immediately conscious of itself; its existence is at once indissolubly subjective and objective, collective and individual. This non-class encompasses all those who have been expelled from production by the abolition of work, or whose capacities are under-employed as a result of the industrialization (in this case, the automation and computerization) of intellectual work. It includes all the supernumeraries of present-day social production, who are potentially or actually unemployed, whether permanently or temporarily, partially or completely. It results from the decomposition of the old society based upon the dignity, value, social utility and desirability of work.[11]

Berman countered this, claiming, 'Marx understands that many people in this working class don't know their address':

> They may not discover who they are, and where they belong, until they are laid-off or fired—or outsourced, or deskilled, or downsized. And other workers, lacking credentials, not dressed so nicely, may not get the fact that many who push them around are really in their class, despite their pretensions, share their vulnerability. How can this reality be put across to people who don't get it, or can't bear it? The complexity of these ideas helped create a new vocation, central to modern society: the *organizer*.

---

[11] André Gorz, *Farewell to the Working Class*, London 1982, p. 68.

But again, this seems a concept from the past, a golden age when labour organizing was a professional occupation—like a photojournalist or a literary critic. But is this still the case today? Doesn't organization some-how organize itself, especially when it really matters? A strength of Shirky's *Here Comes Everybody* is precisely this 'do-it-yourself-with-others' spirit: the idea that grassroots organizing no longer needs a mediator, a Leninist intellectual to reveal 'with sober senses, one's real conditions of life', one's true class status. A lot of people already know this, and even if they do not, they can still manage to organize themselves—or, to some extent, to get organized without consciously knowing it. People create group commonality through face-to-face, 'strong-tie' offline activism, but also through online 'weak-tie' association. The two flanks strengthen one another; the notion of affinity helps the idea of a group to take hold, adding a new dimension: speed—the speed at which crowds assemble and demonstrations take place; the speed at which people of different occupational groups and ages encounter and organize one another.

The spark that triggers any explosive encounter is like that first Jackson Pollock drip: suddenly the paint falls onto the giant canvas; things explode at ground level, on the floor, in the street; dense skeins of black and white swirls disrupt the field of vision; brown and silver nebulae dazzle; paint is layered on swiftly, like meteorites flashing across a white void. There is neither beginning nor end here; entering is via some mid-dle door; there is no meaning other than a pure intensity, a flow of pure becoming. Standing in front of a huge Pollock masterpiece like *One: Number 31* (1950), or *Autumn Rhythm* (1950), shares something of the same dramatic (and unnerving) intensity of standing amid a huge crowd at a demonstration. The same spontaneous energies both incite and terrify; the splattering of colours and entangled lines are there before you. But now they are direct extensions of your own body. Now you are in the canvas. Those swift dripped lines somehow flow through you, become frenzied gestures of your own self in the crowd, the crowd in you. You are simply present here and now; passions are expressed rather than illustrated.

Revolutionary rehearsals

During such intense moments, when people encounter one another, 'the instant of greatest importance', according to Lefebvre, 'is the instant of failure. The drama is situated within that instant of failure: it is the emergence from the everyday or collapse on failing to emerge, it is a caricature or a tragedy, a successful festival or a dubious ceremony.' Therein lies the problem: the encounter 'wants to endure. But it cannot endure (at least, not for very long). Yet this inner contradiction gives it its intensity, which reaches crisis point when the inevitability of its own demise becomes apparent.'[12] One moment leads to another, and a politics of encounter explodes when moments collide, when affinity takes hold. How, then, can the intensity of the encounter be sustained, how can it be harmonized with an authentic politics of transformation, one that endures over the long haul?

In his essay, 'The Nature of Mass Demonstrations', first published when crowds of young men and women piled onto Europe and America's streets in the spring of 1968, John Berger argued that the crowds in demonstrations should be distinguished from crowds in riots or even in revolutionary uprisings. The aim of a crowd in a demonstration was essentially *symbolic*; demonstrations were rehearsals for revolution, but not in a strategic or tactical sense, rather they were 'rehearsals of revolutionary awareness'. A mass demonstration is a spontaneous event; yet it is equally something created by individuals. People come together to create a function, to protest, to affirm; they are not responding to a function, like a crowd of shoppers. The crowd at a demonstration acts rather than reacts; or, if it reacts, it does so in reaction to its own previous actions and how these have been received by the powers that be. Crowds here dramatize the power they still lack: 'The historical role of demonstrations is to show the injustice, cruelty, irrationality of the existing state authority. Demonstrations are protests of innocence.'[13] The crowd that encounters itself at a mass demonstration expresses political ambitions before the political means necessary to realize them are created. The revolutionary in the crowd has to learn how to rehearse symbolically, how to translate inner force into an external, common and transformative praxis; one has to test oneself out in the collective and strategic drama of the historical performance itself.

In his 1972 novel *G*, Berger evoked the experience of the 1898 uprising in Milan, when the cavalry charged the crowd and butchered a hundred workers, wounding many hundreds more:

---

[12] Lefebvre, *Critique of Everyday Life*, vol. 2, London and New York 2002, pp. 351, 345.
[13] John Berger, 'The Nature of Mass Demonstrations', *New Society*, 23 May 1968.

The crowd sees the city around them with different eyes. They have stopped the factories producing, forced the shops to shut, halted the traffic, occupied the streets. It is they who have built the city and they who maintain it. They are discovering their own creativity. In their regular lives they only modify presented circumstances; here, filling the streets and sweeping all before them they oppose their very existence to circumstances. They are rejecting all that they habitually, and despite themselves, accept. Once again they demand together what none can ask alone: Why should I be compelled to sell my life bit by bit so as not to die?[14]

Nobody can know in advance when an epic historical-geographical performance will be enacted, nor are there preconceived formulas for what makes a successful encounter. What is clear, however, is that any moment of encounter will likely be a kind of process without a subject, spreading like wildfire, a moment in which crowds become speedy ensembles of bodies, created via spontaneous online and offline ordering; participants will simultaneously act and react, in a human kaleidoscope in which joy and celebration, violence and wildness, tenderness and abandon somehow get defined. Participants will come together not only as a singularity sharing passions and affirming hopes, but also as a force that creates its own historical space. For the politics of the encounter will always be an encounter *somewhere*, a spatial meeting place. It will always be an illicit rendezvous of human bonding and solidarity, a virtual, emotional and material topography in which something disrupts and intervenes in the paralysis.

What takes hold is what Joyce in *Finnegans Wake* termed a 'collideorscape'.[15] The notion of the encounter is perhaps the central motif of *Finnegans Wake*, and the collideorscape marks for Joyce something of a 'collide and escape', a kaleidoscope of sorts, a coincidence taking hold, shaking things up to give form to another reality; a portmanteau word for a new portmanteau politics. The spatial question will not go away: it will always be the battleground for political struggle, the centre stage of any encounter or collideorscape. But what kind of human—rather than urban—space will this be, and what kind of new social networks hold the key for a 21st-century politics of militant democracy? In what forms will the Joycean *everybuddy*—as *Finnegans Wake* puns, seemingly giving the nod to Facebook addicts everywhere—begin to express itself, as it challenges the crisis-ridden neoliberal order?

---

[14] Berger, *G*, London 1972, pp. 68–9.
[15] Joyce, *Finnegans Wake*, p. 143.

NEW FROM VERSO

THE IDEA OF COMMUNISM

Edited by Costas Douzinas
and Slavoj Žižek

PB • $26.95/£14.99 • 978-1-84467-459-6

A landmark volume gathering contributions on the continuing significance of communism and the need to reconfigure the concept amid contemporary conditions of crisis. With essays by Slavoj Žižek, Alain Badiou, Antoni Negri, Michael Hardt, Jacques Rancière, Terry Eagleton, Jean-Luc Nancy, Susan Buck-Morss, Bruno Bosteels, Peter Hallward, Alberto Toscano and Wang Hui.

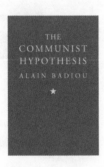

THE COMMUNIST HYPOTHESIS

Alain Badiou

HB • $19.95/£12.99 • 978-1-84467-600-2

'Shaking the foundations of Western liberal democracy'—*Times Higher Education Supplement*

'We know that communism is the right hypothesis. All those who abandon this hypothesis immediately resign themselves to the market economy, to parliamentary democracy—the form of state suited to capitalism—and to the inevitable and "natural" character of the most monstrous inequalities.'

VERSO

JACOB EMERY

ART OF THE

INDUSTRIAL TRACE

S EEN FROM THE air, cultivated expanses of land resemble abstract paintings: the polka-dot patterns produced by agricultural pivots in the American West; the vast electrified grids of cities at night. It is an observation that has been made by many writers and by numerous people in window seats on cloudless days. A major branch of contemporary photography consists of high-altitude panoramas of construction sites, cranberry harvests, strip mines, and so on, rendered legible as objects only through reference to a caption. 'The warm and cool hues of this bauxite waste remind artist J. Henry Fair of a Kandinsky painting,' reads the note to Fair's photograph *Transition*, a gorgeous wash of industrial effluvia typical of his *Industrial Scars* series. Similarly, the photographer Georg Gerster selected views for his aerial photographs 'mostly for their design quality, symmetry of town plans, highways and parking lots, the mosaic patterns of agricultural fields that look like multicoloured patchworks'.[1]

In viewing an object close up, from a great distance, or in a radically new context, we are freed from the straitjacket of automatic recognition and are able to experience it sensuously, as if for the first time. We see industrial infrastructure as art from an aeroplane for the same reason we see a urinal as art in a museum: an accident of perspective might transmute anything into an artistic object. 'Art is a means of experiencing creativity,' Viktor Shklovsky stressed in his 1917 essay, 'Art as Device'. 'The artefact itself is quite unimportant.'[2] This explanation becomes richer when we consider that the defamiliarized vista we see from an aeroplane window suggests the magnitude of the economic system that sustains us and to which we contribute, without ordinarily being sensible of the transformative reach of our activities. In seeing the origin of eggs or the dissemination of electrical power incarnate in a landscape radically altered by human desires and labour, large-scale production appears as creativity in its broadest sense, the realization of will in material.

Yet our aesthetic reaction to this sculptured landscape involves, not just the estranging production of unfamiliarity, but the reproduction of the familiar. The geoglyphic forms below our flight path seem 'like art' because our taste has already been schooled by revolutionaries like Kazimir Malevich, who wrote explicitly of aerial perspective's influence upon the aesthetic of 'space with no horizon' evinced in compositions like his iconic 1915 *Black Square*.[3] *Aeroplane Flying*, his Suprematist composition of the same year, offers an illustration of these principles in its arrangement of black and orange blocks; his subsequent *Head of a Peasant* (1928–32) demonstrates, in the bright geometry of background cropland, the continuity between agricultural forms and his Suprematist experiments, while a formation of aeroplanes in the upper strata of the portrait points to the role of an imagined aerial perspective in the development of that aesthetic. Earthworks pioneer Robert Smithson, whose pieces are themselves often metaphors for the incursions that extraction industries make upon the land, conceived of an artwork that would be viewed from the air as part of a design proposal for a Texas airport; he died in a plane crash in 1973 while surveying a project site.[4] Alongside artists who have openly declared an interest in aerial perspective we might name many more whose forms are more subtly reminiscent of industrialized urbanism or agriculture, like the latticed compositions of Piet Mondrian or the patchy ochre canvases of Mark Rothko.

The patterns of city streets, or blocks of sown and fallow land, are thus already recognizable as artistic forms, forms we have previously encountered on canvas. On another reading, however, the turn

---

[1] J. Henry Fair, *Industrial Scars*, Arts House, Singapore, 19–30 October 2007. On Georg Gerster, see Margaret Dreikausen, *Aerial Perception: Earth as Seen from Aircraft and Spacecraft and Its Influence on Contemporary Art*, Philadelphia 1985, p. 17.

[2] Viktor Shklovsky, *Theory of Prose*, Elmwood Park, IL 1990, p. 6.

[3] John Milner, *Kazimir Malevich and the Art of Geometry*, New Haven 1996, p. 190. For Malevich's own writings on this subject, see especially the essays 'On New Systems in Art/Statics and Speed' (1919) and 'Suprematism' (1924–26), both collected in Kazimir Malevich, *Malevich on Suprematism*, Iowa City 1999.

[4] Smithson, *The Collected Writings*, Berkeley 1996, p. 116. Dreikausen notes that ancient Indian geoglyphs in Ohio and California were rediscovered by aeronauts in the twentieth century: 'Since the figures are of such vast scale, they cannot be recognized from the ground.' *Aerial Perception*, p. 20.

to geometric forms on vast scales suggests not just artists' interest in the estranging potential of aerial perspective, but the conscious or unconscious reproduction in their work of underlying social-historical phenomena: the regularity of mass production or the enormity of the human impact upon our environment. The most compelling materialist theories of art have to do precisely with this sense that art is a meta-phorical expression of the hard historical facts of economic life, with which it advances in tandem.[5] In the most developed forms of this approach—I would cite here Fredric Jameson's *Political Unconscious* and Pierre Macherey's *Theory of Literary Production*—artworks are read as projections or representations of economic life into the surface world of cultural forms, which constitute more or less fragmented and distorted allegories of historical and material forces.[6]

Some version of allegorical materialism seems to be the most compel-ling interpretative strategy available to us at the present time, as it is capable both of accounting for the intuitively felt relationship of neces-sity between economic activity and artistic production—an artist who has nothing to eat cannot live to make art; art develops together with social and technological changes—and of elucidating the content of artworks across the range of media and the spectrum of high and low culture. From this view a Mondrian painting, for example, reflects in its grid-like pattern the very principle of reproducibility inherent in mechanical mass production.

What then do we make of our sense that production practices are, at least as seen from an airplane, somehow already artistic in themselves? The metaphorical relationship between artwork and other kinds of work here

---

[5] For example, Walter Benjamin writes that 'in a film, perception in the form of shocks was established as a formal principle. That which determines the rhythm of production on a conveyer belt is the basis of the rhythm of reception in the film.' *Illuminations*, New York 1968, p. 175.

[6] See Fredric Jameson, *The Political Unconscious: Narrative as a Socially Symbolic Act*, Ithaca, NY 1981, esp. pp. 29–33, comparing superstructural allegory of the base to the medieval system of allegorical exegesis, and pp. 74–102, theorizing the relation of the symbolic levels generated by a cultural text to the ultimate, unnarrativizable horizon of history; and Pierre Macherey, *A Theory of Literary Production*, London 1978, esp. pp. 120–34, a development of Lenin's 1908 observation that Tolstoy, in his contradictory allegiances to peasant culture and the bourgeoisie, unconsciously produced a 'mirror of the Russian Revolution'—a document of a society just barely able to articulate its own internal contradictions, and as yet incapable of conceiving a world in which those conflicts would be superseded.

becomes literal. The artefacts of economic life are not just part of a series of proliferating expressions of the underlying conditions of production, art among them, but are themselves perceived as artistic productions: ploughed furrows and planted crops are works upon the canvas of the globe. This attitude has been most urgently voiced at the fringes of the ideological spectrum and has been especially attractive to the chthonic pretensions of the far right. Martin Heidegger, through metaphors of culture as cultivation, views the artwork as a dialectic between the essential impenetrability of the thing-in-itself, 'the earth', and the subjective 'destiny of a historical people'; art is the revelation of 'the whole' in the relationship between a given culture and its technologically mediated dwelling in a cultivated earth, exampled by Van Gogh's painting of a peasant shoe that contains 'the far-sweeping and ever-uniform furrows of the field.'[7] This approach culminates in the sentimental vision of a people of peasants and craftsmen whose destiny is realized in the landscape—a category implicitly including other peoples, with lesser destinies, who in the paradigmatically agricultural meeting of mute earth and expressive human world are not distinguished from the weeds uprooted, or the earth ripped open by the plough.

On the other hand, the view of art and economy as literally rather than metaphorically identical, albeit with a very different valuation of human agency, is also prominent in the leftist vision of a world historically produced through 'subjection of nature's forces to man, machinery, application of chemistry to industry and agriculture, steam navigation, railways, electric telegraphs, clearing of whole continents for cultivation'—as articulated in the *Communist Manifesto*; Boris Groys has described the attempted realization of this project in the USSR as the 'total art of Stalinism' (*Gesamtkunstwerk Stalin*).[8] Indeed Anatoly Lunacharsky, the Soviet Commissar of Enlightenment until 1929, argued that art and economic development are identical because 'the task of art' is to disclose 'the general laws of artistic taste' and 'apply them to a mechanized industry even more colossal than it is now, to the construction of life and the everyday world'.[9] He conceives industrial production as a form, the ideal form, of poetic activity.

---

[7] Martin Heidegger, *Poetry, Language, Thought*, New York 2001, pp. 47, 54, 33.
[8] Karl Marx and Friedrich Engels, *Marx and Engels: Basic Writings on Politics and Philosophy*, Garden City, NY 1959, p. 12; Boris Groys, *The Total Art of Stalinism: Avant-Garde, Aesthetic Dictatorship, and Beyond*, Princeton, NJ 1992, p. 3.
[9] Anatoly Lunacharsky, *Sobranie sochinenii v vos'mi tomakh*, Moscow 1967, 7.330. English sources cited for all texts when available; otherwise translations are my own.

From his aerial artistic perspective, Lunacharsky's contemporary Malevich foresaw a similar collapse of industry and art, in which 'the green world will be as extinct as the primeval landscape' and 'a new picture is formed by a new aesthetic activity. New animals are born in our modern factories, are coloured according to our taste, and released into the world.'[10] This revolutionary art is not merely a metaphoric image of social life: rather, the farmers and construction workers who reshape the landscape, the genetic engineers who breed livestock 'coloured according to our taste', literally *are* the artists who shape the material of the world. Related attitudes are voiced even now among the artists of global capitalism. Walid Raad, a New York artist who has been instrumental in a boycott of the Abu Dhabi Guggenheim, explained his interest in the working conditions of the museum's builders by appealing to a parallel between two equivalent kinds of work: 'Those working with bricks and mortar deserve the same kind of respect as those working with cameras and paintbrushes.'[11] Artistic and other forms of production are radically collapsed into the single category of labour, an attitude that challenges our conception of the work of art as distinct from other kinds of work.

To approach art as an essentially symbolic projection of material conditions seems inadequate to explain our sense of an artistic dimension to industrial products. Our urge for a perspective from which artwork and other kinds of work are fused into a single phenomenon points to something not quite so naïve as simply seeing the earth as a vast canvas on which human intent daubs its total masterwork. In the following pages, I want to argue that the relevance and aesthetic effect of artworks is not just a matter of their capacity to encode, symbolize, or represent the economic and historical base, but also derives from their status as testaments to the larger economic process in which they participate and of which they are a result; indeed, we recognize artworks as such insofar as they are framed by work of other kinds.

Sign language

One terminology available to us here is Roman Jakobson's definition of communication as the intersection of metaphor—relationships of resemblance and analogy—and metonymy: relationships of contiguity

---

[10] Malevich, *Malevich on Suprematism*, p. 56.
[11] Quoted in Nicolai Ouroussoff, 'Abu Dhabi Guggenheim Faces Protest: Artists Seek to Help Labourers at Museum,' *New York Times*, 17 March 2011.

or causality. Our sense of art as a representation of economic life might be aligned with the metaphoric function, our sense of it as a trace of economic production with the metonymic.[12] Another terminology, which has the advantage of specifically addressing photography, is C. S. Peirce's tripartite classification of signs: the *index*, or 'association by contiguity', refers to its object through a direct connection, as a rolling gait indicates a sailor or the level in a barometer indicates air pressure; the *icon*, or 'association by resemblance', is an image or metaphor which stands in a relationship of likeness or formal analogy to its object; and the *symbol*, or 'intellectual' signification, is the arbitrary, conventional sign—a non-onomatopoeic word, for example.[13] Photography may appear to present an iconic likeness of its object, but Peirce points out that photographs are indexes—the traces of reflected light upon a chemically treated surface. While in certain respects they are 'exactly like the objects they represent', this resemblance is 'due to the photographs having been produced under such circumstances that they were physically forced to correspond point by point to nature.'[14]

The very explanatory force of allegorical readings may blind us to the fact that all work, including the photographic artwork, constitutes a trace of productive activity as well as an image of it. The most sophisticated theories of photography—which are invested in debunking the myth of unmediated photographic evidence in favour of the truth that, as John Tagg puts it, '*every* photograph is the result of specific and, in every sense, significant distortions which render its relation to any prior reality deeply problematic'—tend to understate photography's status as trace of a real object in order to expose how the reproductive medium introduces bias.[15] Yet the truth of Tagg's statement does not prevent us

---

[12] See the 1956 essay 'Two Aspects of Language' in Roman Jakobson, *Language in Literature*, Cambridge, MA 1987, pp. 109–114.
[13] C. S. Peirce, *Philosophical Writings of Peirce*, New York 1955, p. 108. In structuralist parlance these categories correspond to metonymy, metaphor and sign, respectively. Peirce is exemplary in his awareness of their interpenetration, as when he writes that 'it would be difficult, if not impossible, to instance an absolutely pure index, or to find any sign absolutely devoid of the indexical quality' (p. 108), and he perceives semiotic dimensions that might initially surprise us, writing for example that an iconic image like a painting 'is largely conventional in its mode of representation' (p. 105). For a seminal discussion of Peirce's work see Peter Wollen, *Signs and Meaning in the Cinema* [1969], London 1997, Chapter 3.
[14] Peirce, *Philosophical Writings*, p. 106.
[15] John Tagg, *The Burden of Representation: Essays on Photographies and Histories*, Minneapolis 1993, p. 2.

from identifying photographic techniques, like montage and cropping, that distort through context and juxtaposition, as relatively distinct from the distortions introduced by conventional artistic codes or metaphorical operations. Furthermore, it is evident that any product of human activity—from photographic art to fish farming—is involved in and results from the 'prior reality' of economic processes, and can thus be understood as a metonym or index, a consequence or isolated instance of economic activity, as well as a metaphoric or iconic reference to social types and production processes.

This last observation has been the foundation of descriptive sociologies of artistic production, after the fashion of Pierre Bourdieu or Franco Moretti, but I am convinced it has a role to play in interpretation as well. The early works of Dickens, for instance, are structured not just through Victorian ideology, caricatures of social types, and so on, but by the lengths of the chapters, themselves materially determined by the fact that paper was produced thirty-two sheets to a ream.[16] In this sense, the regular plot proportions of *The Pickwick Papers* or *Nicholas Nickleby* are not only a formal allegory of the mechanical productive processes unleashed in England's Industrial Revolution, but the literal trace of those processes. Photography, even if its best theorists have taken pains to show how it is not a transparent testimony to the real, may help us understand how all artworks—even those which, like verbal literature, appear to operate in a wholly conventional and symbolic mode—can be understood as metonymic figures of material life.

When we enjoy from a window seat the electrical grid of Chicago at night or the greens and ochres of Buckinghamshire cropland, we remain within classic aesthetic categories: the beauty of regular proportions, the sublimity of the enormous. But we are also looking at the direct traces of economic activity, of construction crews and harrows. To visualize how persistent these incidental traces can be, consider that the grid of canals and city blocks of an Etrusco-Greek city in Italy can, some two thousand years later, be precisely mapped through the site's lighter and darker shades of marsh grass.[17] Our awareness that the camera is not a natural documentary medium should not blind us to the fact that a photographic image of this archaeological evidence is in itself, as Susan Sontag notes, 'a trace, something directly stencilled off the real, like a

---

[16] Robert L. Patten, *Charles Dickens and His Publishers*, Oxford 1978, p. 55.
[17] Dreikausen, *Aerial Perception*, p. 20.

footprint or a death mask'—'a material vestige of its subject in a way that no painting can be.'[18]

I want ultimately to argue that paintings and novels and music are—in more subtle ways, ways that aerial photography can help us articulate—also interpretable as traces, as photographs are, but also as ploughed land is the evidence of a mode of agricultural production. While all these media are in some sense 'stencilled off the real,' photography explicitly reminds us of the fact, even or especially when those photographs stencil the real but also the unrecognizable, landscapes that might as well be abstract art of the kind in which we typically read only schematic meaning. Rosalind Krauss has taken important steps in this direction by noting that the photograph, as 'a type of icon, or visual likeness, which bears an indexical relationship to its object', has paradoxically become 'the operative model for abstraction' in twentieth-century art.[19] She argues that, by their indexical nature, photographs model an art (for instance, documents of an event or installation) that, in testifying to the existence of the artist and object, only 'repeats the message of pure presence' and therefore requires, to generate other kinds of meaning, the supplemental language of a caption or gloss or biography.

Yet this scheme can be developed in two directions. In the first place, indexes or metonymic figures can in fact encode various kinds of meaning. To use a photographic example, the panoramic juxtaposition of tenements, smokestacks, and graveyard monuments in Walker Evans's 1935 cityscape *Bethlehem* generates an implicit narrative arc involving life, work, and death, and is indeed the precondition of any metaphoric interpretation based on the visual similarity of the chimneys and tombstones: indexical art retains a referential, though not exclusively symbolic, function, and thus produces its own modes of interpretability. In the second place, I question Krauss's conclusion that 'it is the order of the natural world that imprints itself on the photographic emulsion' and that 'the connective tissue binding the objects contained by the photograph is that of the world itself, rather than that of a cultural system', since a world subjected to photographic reproduction cannot be uncomplicatedly 'natural'. Even a document like Man Ray's 1920 emulsion of an accumulation of dust, *Elevage de poussière*, presupposes the

---

[18] Susan Sontag, *A Susan Sontag Reader*, New York 1983, p. 350.
[19] Rosalind Krauss, *The Originality of the Avant-Garde and Other Modernist Myths*, Cambridge, MA 1985, pp. 203, 210–12.

photographic plate on which the dust collects; it is a trace not only of the dust, but of the historically situated artistic medium that articulates its presence. Insofar as human activity and its associated cultural forces have affected everything in the world from the call of starlings to global climate patterns, the world whose 'connective tissue' binds the objects in the photograph is always already implicated in the cultural system.

These points are especially salient in the photographic genre mentioned above, that of aerial images of landscapes so transformed by productive activity that they resemble abstract art. The most widely disseminated examples include the farmland images by Stan Wayman published in *Life*, *National Geographic* photos such as Georg Gerster's and Robert Haas's contour furrows and wastewater pools, and the Jason Hawkes exhibits associated with the BBC television series *Britain from Above*; for instances of explicitly critical works I would cite the aerial photographs of Alex MacLean and Emmet Gowin, J. Henry Fair's *Industrial Scars* and Edward Burtynsky's *Manufactured Landscapes*, and some of the documents made by Robert Smithson. These images of strip mines, bombing ranges, construction sites, factory farmland, fertilizer runoff, sludge piping, and the like are traces of traces, photographic indexes of indexes to economic activity. The objects themselves are identifiable only by reference to the caption; any iconic value of the images is rather their resemblance to abstract painting. J. Henry Fair's panoramas of mine waste and agricultural runoff lack any contextual clues that might allow us to identify their subjects and his prints appear to be 'radiantly colourful abstract canvases'.[20]

In an exposition of cropland images culled from Google Earth, James W. Earl asks us to examine 'the effect produced by plough lines, for example, which resemble the brush strokes of a painter.'[21] While noting the historical ideologies that shape this landscape—the mile-wide intervals crisscrossing America plot Thomas Jefferson's division of the Louisiana Purchase into units suitable for yeoman farmers—Earl also treats objects in this made landscape, like the 'sublime' circles of arable land formed by irrigation pivots, 'as works of art—a kind of folk art, perhaps? Or, if it's too great a stretch to consider the farmers as folk artists, could these be, at the very least, examples of *art trouvé*, found art?' We are close here

---

[20] Porter Anderson, 'Making Art of "Industrial Scars"', CNN, 19 October 2007.
[21] James W. Earl, 'Window Seat: The Art of the Circle Field,' *The Scream Online*, no. 17, May 2010.

to the literalization of agriculture as aesthetic activity manifested in ideologies like the 'total art' of Stalinism or the Heideggerian definition of
the artwork as a 'whole.' But in fact the 'sublime' quality of these images
is not in their total, but rather in their partial nature.

Broken mirrors

Immanuel Kant describes the experience of the sublime as proceeding
from an encounter with that which is larger than we can grasp with
our senses or even imagine.[22] He therefore discounts 'the sublime in
products of art' because we are capable of grasping their purpose intellectually and therefore conceiving the object as a whole despite its scale:
our minds can thus comprehend even the vastness of the pyramids,
while a tsunami still exceeds us. This may be the case if we imagine a
human community in which every individual knows the purpose and
fashioning of every object, as Schiller and Lukács imagined the ancient
Greeks among the products of their handicraft, their pottery and textiles
and stonework. But in fact we inhabit a world of objects, like transistors
and scholarly journals and bauxite slag, whose functioning and purpose
are to the non-specialist opaque, and whose origin is lost within the
vast global movement of commodities. Specialization and class division
arguably prevent any one individual from possessing the sum of knowledge necessary, say, to interpret an artwork.

Thus John Berger writes of Peter Lanyon's abstracted landscape painting *St Just* that the artist 'searches for something that includes a sailor's
knowledge of the coastline, a poacher's knowledge of the cover, a min-
er's knowledge of the seams, a surveyor's knowledge of the contours,
a native's knowledge of the local ghosts, a painter's knowledge of the
light—and yet also something that is contained by none of these.' Due
to the disintegration of society into professions and social classes, the
painting can only be comprehended partially: any sense of it as a 'whole'
depends on information that no audience possesses in its entirety, or is
able to feel as lived experience.[23] London gallery-goers may not fathom
the appalling mine disaster to which the painting refers, while the
miners may be unable to decode the painting's abstracted surface. In

---

[22] Immanuel Kant, *Critique of Judgment*, Amherst, NY 2000, pp. 109–10, 113.
[23] John Berger, 'Landscapes and Close-ups', *New Statesman*, 3 April 1954. Berger
complains of the resultant 'lack of any integrated attitude to Nature,' which drives
Lanyon, in his effort to transcend this lack, 'to discover his own symbolism which
is then inevitably over-vague and incomprehensible.'

referring its viewers to a caption, the painting admits itself incomplete, insufficient as a representation of the landscape. This insufficiency only makes legible our perennial condition as inhabitants of an economic system that exceeds our comprehension, as Rebecca West writes in 1941 of 'that vast suspension bridge which always troubles me because it reminds me that in this mechanized age I am as little able to understand my environment as any primitive woman who thinks that a waterfall is inhabited by a spirit.'[24] The reality of the global economy, which exists precisely through specialization, segregation, and division of labour, can only be represented as a fragment, trace, or obviously reduced model.[25]

The index is, therefore, a necessary mode of referring to economic activity in art, in photography *per se* but also in media like Robert Smithson's *Non-Sites*: crushed rock from extraction pits, framed in boxes or arranged on shelves, operates as synecdoche of the earth, of the mine, of the extraction industry in general. 'How can one contain this 'oceanic' site?' Smithson writes of his experience in a Pennsylvania slate quarry.[26] Discussing Burtynsky's more explicitly environmentally engaged series *Manufactured Landscapes*, Kenneth Baker draws our attention to the artist's

> oblique but insistent emphasis on what the camera inevitably excludes. There, if anywhere, lies the truth that is left to photography in the contemporary world: it accurately mirrors not the way things work, but our thunderstruck incapacity to comprehend the total world system . . . We may glimpse local spectacles and calamities, but never see the situation whole. The occasional open horizons in 'Shipbreaking', 'Nickel Tailings' and 'Oil Refineries' remind us of the vast distances across which industries in the global economy interconnect.[27]

Burtynsky's *Railcuts*, for example—sheer surfaces of blasted rock with the single horizontal line of a train track running across the face of the stone—testify to the scope of the global transportation network that

---

[24] Rebecca West, *Black Lamb and Grey Falcon*, London 1994, p. 15.

[25] Schiller anticipates this idea that division of labour prevents modern humans from perceiving the social whole: 'The image of the human species is projected in magnified form into separate individuals—but as fragments, not in different combinations, with the result that one has to go the rounds from one individual to another in order to be able to piece together a complete image of the species.' Friedrich Schiller, *Essays*, New York 2005, p. 99.

[26] Robert Smithson, *Collected Writings*, Berkeley 1996, p. 111.

[27] Kenneth Baker, 'Form Versus Portent: Edward Burtynsky's Endangered Landscapes', in *Manufactured Landscapes: The Photographs of Edward Burtynsky*, by Lori Pauli and Edward Burtynsky, Ottawa 2003, p. 44.

sustains us and which we serve, but they do so in necessarily partial fashion. The source and destination of that line, which dissolves beyond the picture into the strip mines, factory lots, and refuse heaps of Burtynsky's other images, are literally unrepresentable.

In its ironic contrast of the totality that exceeds our perception and our finite, overwhelmed impression of the object, the sublime necessarily involves the synecdoche, the fragment, the trace. Macherey compares artistic text to a broken mirror: 'The relationship between the mirror and what it reflects (the historical reality) is partial: the mirror selects, it does not reflect everything. The selection itself is not fortuitous, it is symptomatic; it can tell us about the nature of the mirror.'[28] He has in mind the ideological blind spots that disclose for us the biases of the text in which they are manifest, but this inability to provide a complete picture reflects upon the world that is represented as well as the text that represents it, and which becomes in the same stroke a part of that world. We can note the iconic functions of Burtynsky's photographs—as representations, emblematic types, or images of abstract painting in another medium—as well as the symbolic ones: historically determined conventions of representation and interpretation, for example. But much of their relevance and indeed of their aesthetic effect derives from their value as testaments to a larger process, one whose magnitude is beyond our individual understanding and is for that reason more pressing than we can even imagine.

Reclamations

Fair and Burtynsky's most striking images are often of metal tailings—the iridescent slurry retained on mining sites both as toxic waste and as resource stockpile, should commodity prices rise high enough to warrant reprocessing—while many earthworks, from Harvey Fite's *Opus 40* (begun in 1938) to Vik Muniz's *Pictures of Earthwork* (2005–06), have utilized mines as project locations. The suitability of mine sites for large-scale earthworks and the striking qualities of tailings as a medium enable a marriage of convenience between art and industry. Robert Smithson entered into negotiations with several mining companies on reclamation projects, in one case generating designs for a spiralling system of holding ponds for copper tailings, and expressed his hope for an artistically mediated 'dialectic between mining and land reclamation'—

---

[28] Macherey, *Theory of Literary Production*, p. 120.

'such devastated places as strip mines could be recycled in terms of earth art.'[29] However, artist Daniel Buren (who has criticized Smithson for fleeing the gallery on exotic 'artistic safaris') has argued that the capitalist system supports art precisely because art functions to conceal and protect the frames—whether understood as ideology, the gallery system, or the literal location of the artwork—that contain it: 'This is what the dominant ideology wants, that what is contained should provide, very subtly, a screen for the container.'[30] Speaking at the dedication of a reclamation project in Washington State, Robert Morris bitterly envisioned an earth art ideologically assimilated into the extraction industry, making it possible 'to rip up the landscape for one last shovelful of a non-renewable energy source if an artist can be found (cheap, mind you) to transform the devastation into an inspiring and modern work of art.'[31] The art of earthwork or the industrial trace suggests that any exploitation might be socially redeemed through its transmutation into art—rendering earth art an economic commodity at the very moment industry becomes legible as aesthetic text.

In relation to the larger economy, reclamation art thus appears as something like the play-within-the-play in *Hamlet*, which both reproduces the enclosing tragedy's themes and actions and acts out a determining role in its plot development—the species of *mise en abîme* or internal text which, according to Yuri Lotman, in symbolizing the framing work not only 'becomes a part of the text but also transforms the text in which it is included.'[32] In mapping the artist's experience of the mine, the earthwork is defined through and against its origin, and even physical framing, deep within the larger work of industrial excavation. Insofar as it shares a location, a scale and even a paymaster with the rest of the extraction process, earth art is otherwise rendered qualitatively identical to the exploitation of resources with which it is so intimately involved both as icon and as index. The artwork here becomes recognizable as

---

[29] Smithson, *Collected Writings*, p. 379. On Smithson's involvement in mine ecology see Ron Graziani, *Robert Smithson and the American Landscape*, Cambridge 2004, pp. 151–8.

[30] Quoted and discussed in Craig Owens, *Beyond Recognition: Representation, Power, and Culture*, Berkeley 1992, p. 130.

[31] Quoted in John Beardsley, *Earthworks and Beyond*, New York 2006, p. 44.

[32] Yuri Lotman, *Kul'tura i vzryv*, Moscow 1992, p. 113. To make a comparison to economics in its strictest sense, the effect is something like the Euro currency, seen on the one hand as a symbol of the economic cohesion of the European Union, on the other as a policy tool that will bring about European unity by implementing a common market.

such solely through its relationship to the industrial work that frames it, which it both conceals and exposes by simulating industrial processes within the depths of the site. Although itself a kind of paid work on an industrial scale, the reclamation project as art allows us to recognize the mine itself as a cultural phenomenon: Lucien Dällenbach has observed that a *mise en abîme* serves to define the framing text as text, just as *Hamlet*'s play-within-the-play reminds the spectator of the theatricality of *Hamlet* itself.[33] Related dynamics occur in non-visual media such as music—most obviously in the genre of industrial rock, a moniker literalized by groups like Einstürzende Neubauten, or 'Collapsing New Buildings.' Their composition 'Autobahn', performed in 1983 on a Berlin road construction site, begins with the sound of a shovel scraping in the earth and adds in an array of tools and building materials repurposed as instrumentation: the piece testifies powerfully to the constructedness—and ongoing re-construction—of the city and of its sonic environment.

Smithson criticized the practice of idealistically 'representing nature one step removed in lyric poetry and landscape painting' in favour of an earth art which does not ignore or reject the dialectic between the land and its workers, but which rather recognizes itself as a species of productive work: 'The best sites for "earth art" are sites that have been disrupted by industry, reckless urbanization, or nature's own devastation . . . Such land is cultivated or recycled as art.'[34] Art, traditionally conceptualized as a diversion from utilitarian aims—an amphora is made legible as art only by being emptied of its use-value, its contents of oil or wine, and placed on display—becomes reconceptualized here as a work in the raw material of waste, the recuperation of industrial by-products or waste land as an integral part of the cultural and economic system. Perhaps the most universally recognizable earthwork, Smithson's *Spiral Jetty*, was constructed near an abandoned oil jetty in Utah's Great Salt Lake; the artist referred to the piece variously as the cultivation of a dead sea and as a reclamation site, and the juxtaposition of artwork and extraction site deliberately points to 'artworks as part of a larger set of cultural interventions in the land'.[35]

---

[33] Lucien Dällenbach, *The Mirror in the Text*, Oxford 1989, p. 57.
[34] Smithson, *Collected Writings*, pp. 164–5.
[35] Smithson, *Collected Writings*, pp. 165, 380; Chris Taylor and Bill Gilbert, *Land Arts of the American West*, Austin 2009, p. 150.

If these earthworks, through their location as well as through their industrial forms and scale, draw attention to the incursions of extraction industries into a marked landscape, seed and crop arts, for all their commodified folksy nostalgia, similarly present us with industrial technology writ large. Since 1993, the Japanese village of Inakadate has created vast annual tableaux of mountainscapes, samurai, and mounted generals out of different strains of planted rice.[36] Although iconically representing preindustrial history and idealized scenes of nature, this art *indicates* much more: it bears traces, for instance, of the computer modelling used to project the image (perspectivized to be viewed from the town's central tower), and of the science of genetic engineering, responsible not only for the Monsanto monocultures of commercial farms but for the red, yellow, and white rices planted in these pictures alongside the two local varieties. Indeed, this uniquely rural genre points directly to the economic decline of rural Japan, which the rice images are supposed to overcome by attracting tourists, stemming population loss, and ultimately transforming the old agricultural community into a new 'art village' whose medium is agriculture. The mainstay of the local economy remains rice, grown no longer as foodstuff but as artwork, and on a similarly communal scale: in the spring of 2010, 1,200 villagers contributed labour to the *tanbo* image of a samurai and warrior monk. Plans to include a Japan Airways logo in 2008 were narrowly scotched, but the close link between products made into images and images made into products is testified in the works of the American crop artist Stan Herd, whose best-known—and best-remunerated—works include a vast Absolut Vodka advertisement in clover, wheat, and sorghum and the gigantic Buick automobile featured in a 1992 Super Bowl commercial.

Wasted lives

Most of the artworks discussed above—photographs, earthworks, crop art—omit the signature, the index of authorship we look to in order to authenticate an artwork. But James W. Earl notes of an irrigation circle at harvest time that a farmer backtracked over his work in order, using his tractor wheels as a stylus, to write out his name in cursive visible from a Google satellite: 'John'. 'Is this man proud of his work?' writes Earl.

---

[36] Martin Fackler, 'Japanese Village Creates Art from Hues of Rice', *New York Times*, 25 July 2010.

'Is he really signing it, as an artist would?'[37] To idealize the worker as an eager artist, fulfilled in his awareness of his labour, is not only largely untrue but also buys into the dogma that in 'loving our work' we find self-realization, rather than embrace our alienation. Yet there may be a kernel of truth in our urge to discover a perspective from which every work is a work of art, the signatory mark of our species upon the landscape we have made. There is indeed a sense in which humanity is the transcendental author of a global work that in turn authors us. As Raymond Williams noted, the economic base is much more than the heavy industry stressed to the exclusion of other factors by dogmatic Marxism, because 'the most important thing a worker ever produces is himself, himself in the fact of that kind of labour, or the broader historical emphasis of men producing themselves, themselves and their history.'[38]

From this point of view, the material world we produce is not only our work, it is a cultural text, our history-in-progress—a collective, deeply encoded autobiography. For we become ourselves only through our ongoing production of a world that continually produces us. 'In taking food, for example, the human being produces his own body,' writes Marx, but 'the hunger gratified by cooked meat eaten with a knife and fork is a different hunger from that which bolts down raw meat with the aid of hand, nail, and tooth . . . Production thus creates the consumer.'[39] Even our sense of aesthetics develops in dialectic with material aesthetic objects, since 'the object of art—like every other product—creates a public which is sensitive to art and enjoys beauty. Production thus not only creates an object for the subject, but also a subject for the object.' We are again on the territory of the *mise en abîme*, since to say that every artwork simultaneously represents and acts upon its viewer's world reiterates the observations made above about industrial traces as aesthetic texts framed against the larger work of economic life—even if Marx himself, at his historical moment, would not have recognized the aesthetic dimension in those objects.

Many of the most obviously indexical documents of modern art foreground an autobiographical or signatory function. Dennis Oppenheimer's 1975 earthwork *Identity Stretch*, a vast image of his own thumbprint sculpted in furrows of asphalt across a hazardous waste disposal site

---

[37] Earl, 'Window Seat'.
[38] Raymond Williams, *Culture and Materialism*, London 1980, p. 35.
[39] Marx, *Grundrisse*, London 1993, pp. 90–1.

in Lewiston, New York, operates as an illiterate mark of the self upon the toxic by-products of the industrial system. More recently, Tim Noble and Sue Webster have created sculptures of trash which, when properly lit, project crisp images of the artists onto the wall behind. One of these self-portraits, *Dirty White Trash (With Gulls)*, is made of six months of household refuse and represents the artists sitting back to back, one of them smoking a cigarette and the other drinking a glass of wine. But the artists are not here resting; rather, by depicting themselves in the act of consumption, they are representing their production of the trash of which the image is a point-to-point projection: they are going about the business of their everyday lives, to be sure, but they are also generating the cigarette butts and bottles of which the sculpture is prominently composed. We are tempted to say in these instances that the recognizable image of human beings is the trace, in light and shadow, of the arrangement of rubbish, but in fact it is just as accurate to say it is the pile of trash that is a trace, a document of the artists' consumption and self-production.

The autobiography of the human species we discern in landscapes reveals the quixotic nature of any effort to elucidate an artwork exclusively as allegorical. Framed landscapes—whether Robert Smithson's or farmer John's—exceed metaphoric understanding not merely because, as miniature models or typical examples of larger economic and historical phenomena, they are necessarily reduced and partial, but because they are legible only through indexical reference to ourselves as authors, our contribution to and formation within the economic system we seek to grasp through representation and interpretation. Yet our experience of this transformed landscape can lead us, not to a hyperbolic 'total art', but into a series of dynamic interpretative processes. Metonymy operates as a tonic against the totalizing impulse of metaphoric identity—an identity which, at the moment we wholly accept it, becomes ideology, the internalized error that prevents us, in our complacency, from realizing what knowledge we possess.

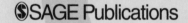

REVIEWS

Patrick Wilcken, *Claude Lévi-Strauss: The Poet in the Laboratory*
Bloomsbury: London 2010, £30, hardback
375 pp, 978 0 7475 8362 2

PERRY ANDERSON

THE MYTHOLOGIAN

The twentieth century's most famous anthropologist might well intimidate any prospective biographer. Claude Lévi-Strauss, who died two years ago, denied that he possessed any individuality of interest. He could remember little of his own past, he said, and did not even feel he had written his own books. He was just a 'passive crossroads' where 'things happened'— 'I never had, and still do not have, the perception of feeling my personal identity. I appear to myself as the place where something is going on, but there is no "I", no "me"'. Nor were such claims mere personal avowals. His intellectual system was based on a radical dismissal of the significance, even reality, of the subject. Such a double barrier might seem obstacle enough to a biography. But it could be thought to rear still higher from the fact that Lévi-Strauss was also, paradoxically, the author of a memoir, *Tristes Tropiques*, by any reckoning a literary masterpiece, in which he set down what he represented as the decisive experiences of his life. Who could hope to improve on it? Certainly no conventional chronicler. In Francophone culture, where the art of biography has long been noticeably weak, the one attempt at a full-length portrait, by Denis Bertholet in 2003, is testimony enough to that.

Patrick Wilcken has defied every such difficulty. *Claude Lévi-Strauss: The Poet in the Laboratory* is both a biography and a critical study of the thinker at the highest level. Graceful and vivid as a narrative, it is also a model of intellectual judgement. Free equally of any impulse to revere or temptation to debunk, Wilcken has produced a beautifully calm, clear-eyed account of the life and thought of his subject. The story he tells can be divided into five parts. Born in 1908, son of a soon *démodé* painter and musical enthusiast, in his youth Lévi-Strauss was an active socialist. Attracted to the arts, he was trained in philosophy, at a time of avant-garde ferment and lack of rigid disciplinary boundaries. His first published article was on Babeuf, his dissertation on Marxism. At the age of twenty-six, then teacher at a provincial lycée, he was suddenly offered the chance of joining a small group of French scholars— Braudel was another—to provide instruction at the recently founded University of São Paulo. The patron of this call was his former supervisor, the sociologist Célestin Bouglé, an associate of Durkheim, and the post he chose to occupy at São Paulo was in sociology. He would later open *Tristes Tropiques* with the celebrated words: 'I hate travelling and explorers'. But these were strictly for effect. Bored and restless in France, like many intellectuals of his generation (Malraux and Nizan had already made their names with exploits abroad), elsewhere Lévi-Strauss more truthfully confessed: 'I was in a state of intense intellectual excitement. I felt I was reliving the adventures of the first sixteenth-century explorers. I was discovering the New World for myself. Everything seemed mythical: the scenery, the plants, the animals'.

Here Wilcken, the author of a fine study of the Portuguese court in Rio, has the enormous advantage of an intimate knowledge of the country where Lévi-Strauss landed. For the first time, the experience that transformed him into an anthropologist is more properly contextualized. In France, the sociology of Durkheim and then of Mauss extended indifferently across modern to 'primitive'—i.e pre-literate—societies, as the more historically minded work of Weber or Sombart in Germany did not. Ethnology was more a loose province of sociology than a distinct discipline. Study of local tribes was thus in a sense the obvious direction for Lévi-Strauss to go, if he was to capitalize on his time in Brazil for advancement at home. He was still drawn to the arts— he and his wife were soon frequenting the milieu around Mário de Andrade, Brazil's leading modernist poet, with whom the couple became good friends; and he still nurtured political ambitions—though indifferent to the local scene, where a Communist rising exploded shortly after his arrival, and a dictatorship modelled on the regimes of Salazar and Mussolini was installed not long after. In 1936, when the Popular Front came to power at home, he was disappointed not to receive any summons from a Socialist ministry in Paris. It was then that he decided to abandon the idea of a political career. Ethnographic exploration of the Brazilian interior became the alternative.

With the publication of *Tristes Tropiques* twenty years later, forays to the Caduveo, the Bororo and the Nambikwara became the stuff of legend. Wilcken's meticulous reconstruction of these sorties, cool but never unsympathetic, shows the reality. By contemporary standards, these were brief, itinerant visitations, involving as much guess-work as field-work in a modern sense. Not even very conversant with Portuguese, Lévi-Strauss knew no Indian language, and spent no extended time with any of the native groups whom he encountered. Nor was his principal expedition, in 1938, at all like the solitary pilgrimage tacitly suggested by his memoir. In Wilcken's words:

> When the crew and equipment were finally assembled on fields on the out-skirts of Cuiabá, the herds of pack animals, the boxes, bags and saddles, the bearded men in loose cotton shorts and leather boots looked more like a travelling country fair than a scientific expedition. In the pages of *Tristes Tropiques*, this large supporting cast often vanishes into the background. In reality, the Serra do Norte expedition was as far from the Malinowskian eth-nographic gold standard—the early-twentieth-century loner, painstakingly learning the local language, submerging himself in their culture—as was possible. In contrast to the Conradesque journey to the extremes of human-ity, much of the time Lévi-Strauss's entourage would outnumber the natives he was trying to study.

But Wilcken is not censorious. Whatever its other shortcomings, the expedition was not only complicated and hazardous, but productive, furnishing Lévi-Strauss with a store of imaginative conjectures that would stand him in good stead when he got to his real terrain of enquiry, thousands of miles from scrub or jungle. Back in France in the spring of 1939, just turned thirty, his mind still occupied with what he had seen, he was now so depoliticized that he was oblivious not only to the imminence of war in Europe, but to the realities of Nazi victory and Vichy collaboration in 1940, attempting—if fortunately failing—to move back to occupied Paris as a teacher when Jews were already at risk. Fired under Pétain, denied a return visa to Brazil, he secured an invitation from the New School, and (assisted by the wealthy con-nexion of an aunt in the US), set sail from Marseilles in a boat whose other refugees included André Breton and Victor Serge, depicted in one of the most piquant episodes of *Tristes Tropiques*. Eventually arriving in New York, Manhattan was, as Wilcken rightly comments, more than the Mato Grosso, 'his true culture shock'.

Here, amid an expatriate French community far larger than in São Paulo, he became embedded in an avant-garde milieu of surrealists—Max Ernst, Yves Tanguy, André Masson, Roberto Matta, not to speak of Breton himself—that took anthropology along with psychoanalysis as keys to the unconscious springs of existence. He had painted as a boy; in Brazil, he had started to write a play in the spirit of Corneille; in France, to compose a novel in the style of Conrad. In New York, he gave up such ambitions, but learnt how to invest the sensibility behind them (now inflected by this setting: 'the surrealists enriched and refined my aesthetic tastes') in forms that would be discursive rather than creative.

The decisive change, however, came from two other directions: exposure to the empirical wealth of American ethnology, much of it assembled by Franz Boas, still alive in New York, and to the theoretical outlook of Prague linguistics, brought to America by Roman Jakobson, who became a close friend. Neither was familiar in France. Settling down to master the first in the New York Public Library, Lévi-Strauss absorbed the second as the fundamental framework of his thought thereafter. Some seven years later—he was now the post-war French cultural attaché, in a palatial mansion on Fifth Avenue—his fusion of the two yielded *The Elementary Structures of Kinship*, which appeared soon after his return to Paris in 1948. In this huge compendium, which sought to formalize a vast array of marriage systems in the known pre-literate world into a set of inter-related patterns, he argued that the taboo on incest was an anthropological universal, marking the break from nature to culture that made possible human society. Although by no means all of the findings on which the book was based were accurate, nor its interpretations always reliable, nothing like *Elementary Structures* had been attempted before. In Wilcken's words: 'Its originality, the confidence of its assertions, the sense of a long overdue theoretical reorientation, made it the landmark publication of its times.' The bulk of it might seem impenetrably technical, but its central thesis was readily intelligible—strikingly so. It would be some decades before its basic premise would be shown to be wrong: historically, there was no universal prohibition on incest, some societies—Ancient Persia, Egypt—even enjoining it.

When *Elementary Structures* came out, Lévi-Strauss was still, academically speaking, an outsider in France. The public fortune of the book was made by a glowing review of it in *Les Temps modernes* by Simone de Beauvoir, once a fellow student of Lévi-Strauss, who had consulted the manuscript while writing *The Second Sex*. Its academic acceptance was slower. Twice denied a chair at the Collège de France, Lévi-Strauss shifted his focus from kinship to myths, and in 1952 published his first essay aimed directly at a wider audience, *Race and History*. In it, he deflated Western pretensions to cognitive superiority over pre-literate societies; the arrival of modern industry and science as the outcome of chance combinations at the roulette table of time, rather than any inner historical dynamic. Three years later came the revelation of his exceptional literary gifts, with the sombre fireworks of *Tristes Tropiques*—a philosophical meditation as much as, or more than, an anthropological memoir. Under the sign of Lucretius and Rousseau rather than of Durkheim, it staged his time in Brazil as a relentless destruction of romantic illusions, that was yet also a fabulous rite of passage to truths about humanity and its place in the universe, repressed by metropolitan hubris. Of his second, and more significant, formation as an ethnologist in New York, he said nothing. For method, he professed to three 'mistresses', Marx, Freud and Geology, each exploring hidden strata below the surface of reality. In 1955, this was a credo that did nothing to diminish the appeal of his book. Unanimously, and understandably, *Tristes Tropiques* was hailed as a classic of French letters.

In these years, it is striking how close were the ties—paradoxical though this might seem, given the antagonism between structuralism and existentialism—linking Lévi-Strauss to the powerhouse of left culture led by Sartre. Not only did de Beauvoir go out of her way to put *Elementary Structures* on the map. It was also in *Les Temps modernes* that a pre-publication chapter of *Tristes Tropiques* appeared, as did such well-known later texts as 'La Geste d'Asdiwal'. Lévi-Strauss's eventual entry into the Collège de France, ten years after his first attempt, was orchestrated by Merleau-Ponty. A sense of where influence lay no doubt played a part in this, for Lévi-Strauss. But it was also an intellectual configuration not untypical of the Fourth Republic, marked by often unpredictable alliances and sustained, impassioned debates which would abruptly decline under the Fifth. With that change of regime, structuralism proper was born. In 1959, Lévi-Strauss published its manifesto, in the collection of essays entitled *Structural Anthropology*. 'For centuries the humanities and social sciences have resigned themselves to contemplating the world of the natural and exact sciences as a kind of paradise which they will never enter', he declared, but 'suddenly there is a small door which is being opened between the two fields and it is linguistics that has done it.' Not only myths or folktales, but in principle any phenomena of the social or cultural world, could henceforth be mapped and decoded with the rigour of phonemes. Since Comte, French thought had always contained a significant strand of scientism. In broadcasting an anthropology equipped with the authority of linguistics, Lévi-Strauss bid to make it dominant.

For a season, he did so with considerable success, as one enterprising spirit after another strove to emulate or extend his programme across a wide range of fields, while he consolidated its hegemony from his command post at the apex of French learning. In a virtuoso performance, *The Savage Mind* (1962) set out to show at once the innate structuralism of the classificatory systems of pre-literate societies, and the futile pretensions of Marxism—let alone existentialism—in the person of Sartre, to represent any advance on them. This was a theoretical edifice, however, resting on a frail foundation: the notion that language offered an analogy for the study of any other domain of social life. Saussure himself, the originator of structural linguistics, had expressly warned against this illusion. But much as the new genetics today has spawned a host of hopeful applicants of evolutionary theory to every conceivable field of the humanities and social sciences, regardless of the lack of any other than a metaphorical connexion between them, so half a century ago linguistics captivated a wide array of enthusiasts as the Open Sesame to an understanding of the world at large. Lévi-Strauss's own contribution to this expansion was his monumental tetralogy on the myth-systems of the Americas, *Mythologiques* (1964–1971): some two thousand pages purporting to lay bare universal properties of the human mind, identical in myths and their analyst, unfolded by him in a scientific composition, melodic and self-referential as music.

By the end of the seventies, the structuralist wave had ebbed, and eventually, Lévi-Strauss himself drew back from the extravagances he had helped to launch, remarking—fifteen years after *The Savage Mind*—that structuralism was no more than a 'very faint and pale imitation of what the hard sciences are doing'. He had, he said, simply been trying to find some kind of order behind apparent disorder in his materials, without imposing any conclusions on them. More pronounced than any theoretical retraction, perhaps only tactical, was a political and cultural regression. In old age, the one-time sympathizer with socialism and surrealism became increasingly conservative—a pillar of the Académie Française, disliker of modern art, electoral moderate, admirer of Gobineau. Still, these were background preferences, on which Lévi-Strauss did not greatly insist. The subsequent star of structuralism inverted this trajectory, but to no better intellectual effect— Foucault moving with scarcely a pause from a 'new philosophy' welcome at the Elysée, to a 'people's justice' preached at the Gauche Prolétarienne. Lévi-Strauss certainly knew how to fan coverage of his ideas, and advance his own interests, but he did so within the limits of a certain traditional reserve and old-fashioned dignity. The younger man's exhibitionist pirouettes and hunger for publicity were foreign to him. Aware how arbitrary were Foucault's archaeologies, he declined any institutional support for his admirer.

The final verdict of Wilcken's delicate and moving book is impeccable. 'In a world of ever more specialized areas of knowledge, there may never again be a body of work of such exhilarating reach and ambition', but though 'there was great breadth and scope to Lévi-Strauss's ideas', they were ultimately fitted into an 'intellectually claustrophobic space'—a 'one-man enterprise that became so utterly idiosyncratic that it was impossible to build on.' As a system, 'structuralism implied depth, but with its interplay of referentless signs, often felt more like skidding along polished glass.' Yet 'what gave life to Lévi-Strauss's output, and introduced the lyricism that baffled his Anglo-Saxon critics, was a profound interest in aesthetic expression and appreciation that ran in tandem with the cognitive side of his work.' The anthropologist saw himself as an artist *manqué*. But Lévi-Strauss was not only a great collector and weaver of narratives—'myths are very beautiful objects', he remarked, 'and one never tires of contemplating them, manipulating them'. The second verb tells its own story. He was also a great writer, in the art, no minor one, of rhetoric.

Uwe Tellkamp, *Der Turm*
Suhrkamp: Frankfurt 2008, €24.80, hardback
976 pp, 978 351 842 020 1

FREDRIC JAMESON

DRESDEN'S CLOCKS

Anyone with a commitment to socialism needs to take an interest in the history and fate of the German Democratic Republic (DDR), up to now the object of systematic neglect by West-of-the-Rhine liberal and radical intellectuals alike, who have scant knowledge of its achievements in painting and film, and assume its economic and political lessons to be exclusively negative. This is yet another instance in which Cold War dismissals in the name of Stalinism and totalitarianism—essentially political judgements—continue to be tacitly accepted by today's lefts in embarrassed silence. To be sure, the Soviet Union is another matter, and its rise and fall is as respectable a historical topic as the life and death of the Roman Empire; but at the same time it is widely assumed that the evolution of its 'satellites' is necessarily a secondary matter.

Yet Germany was the very heartland of Marxism, with the largest party in Europe, its leaders and intellectuals the most enlightened and committed of such formations anywhere; comparable to the prestige of the Italian Communist Party after World War Two. It is not to be assumed that the German survivors who returned from Moscow after the war to found a new socialist state were mere puppets of the Russians (however unattractive we may find Ulbricht's character). On the contrary, there were probably proportionately fewer opportunists among these believers than in the minority parties of the other Eastern states. Meanwhile, as the only socialist country besides Korea to share a border and a language with a capitalist counterpart, and as the object of the most intensive Western strategy of obstruction and sabotage outside Cuba, East Germany—virtually levelled to the ground and its own diminished population drowned in German-speaking refugees from further east—faced problems unparalleled in other socialist experiments since the early years of the Soviet Union itself.

Meanwhile, the disgrace of the wholesale privatization of collective assets after 'the fall' was matched only by the crimes of the oligarchs in the soon-to-be ex-Soviet Union. As for culture, after Brecht, only literature in which 'dissidence' (a late 70s term) could be detected was of any interest abroad, the daily life of the DDR constituting for the West little more than one long life sentence or waste of time. The absorption of this aberrant entity back into the Bundesrepublik was thereby seen as a simple return to normality, with the exception, to be sure, of economic normality—production, employment and the like.

This is the situation in which we may well wish to take note of the appearance of what has seemed to some the most considerable work of East German literature, Uwe Tellkamp's massive novel *Der Turm* (The Tower). The book appeared three years ago in what I am still tempted to call West Germany to enormous acclaim, winning all the literary prizes and catapulting its author at once to the summit of the current German pantheon. The scandalous unfamiliarity of this author's name is only partly due to the absence of an English translation (as far as I know, it has only been translated into Dutch and Italian); probably the lack of interest in the DDR is just as significant, and—despite Susan Sontag's naive questioning of the very existence of a 'second-world literature'—publishers have understood that, after the end of the Cold War, there is little enough public demand here for accounts of everyday socialism. Still, I call this work by a forty-year-old writer who grew up in the DDR an 'East German novel' because it is saturated by that daily life, so different from our own, and has an authenticity unavailable even in the finest imaginative descriptions by outsiders, such as Günther Grass's remarkable *Ein weites Feld*; let alone the punk literature of younger Eastern writers who have never lived in the system that formed their elders. Meanwhile, to be sure, Tellkamp's is an extraordinary and demanding art with a sentence-density comparable only to Thomas Mann or Grass himself (in German; in other languages Proust or Faulkner might be distant reference points); while his narrative experimentation, although by no means as complex as that of earlier East German writers such as Uwe Johnson or Heiner Müller, has all the maturity of traditional modernist virtuosity.

Even German readers, however, have complained of the length (a thousand pages), of which, as one critic put it, only the last one-fifth—the disintegration of the East German state—has any genuine, if muffled, narrative excitement. And it is certain that the temporal focus of this work, which begins with Marx's centenary (and Brezhnev's death) in 1983 and ends in November 1989, demands a painstaking and detailed laying in place of the daily life of its protagonists in order all the more accurately to show its dissolution.

So the first part of the book is necessarily iterative, in Genette's sense of specifically situated scenes which are, nevertheless, designed to show how it always was, what they always did (Combray on a Saturday or Sunday morning). This makes for an episodic series of sketches of apartment life, school, publishers' meetings and official encounters with the ideological 'central committee' of the region; of parties and of vacations at Party establishments on the Baltic Coast; glimpses of *Haushaltungstag* (when bachelors are given time off to do the cleaning), hospital routines, the brief East–West contact of the Leipziger Buchmesse, and so forth. 'Only the exhaustive is truly interesting', said Thomas Mann; and it will be a central question for us whether such loving detail constitutes what is today identified as *Ostalgie*—nostalgia for an 'actually existing socialism' that has vanished.

But we must be careful not to grasp Genette's technical concept in any oversimplified way; to be sure, on the one hand, the iterative constitutes a solution to the older way of summarizing past events and their 'uneventful' continuities. But it is not necessarily—or at least, not in this novel—the opposite number to the Event, the vivid representation of things finally happening; or to the real time of change and history as we might be tempted to imagine it emerging from the breakdown of a seemingly rather static system. 'There is no misfortune other than that of not being alive,' cries Christa Wolf at the conclusion of her Stasi-novella *Was bleibt*. 'And in the end, no desperation other than that of not having lived.' But that is not my impression of living in *Der Turm*; and we will have to wait for its sequel to know what 'real life' lies beyond it.

At any rate, events here—and on their presence turns the very status of *Der Turm* as a historical novel—take place off stage; and, in a society as yet uncolonized by the modern media, they are transmitted in gossip and as rumour, as what takes place outside and beyond daily life, but also as what requires no explanation: Bitterfeld 1959, Chernobyl, the meaning of the presence of both German leaders at the reopening of the rebuilt Dresden opera house, Andropov's death, Father Popieliuszko, the Central Committee's suspicions of the new Soviet leadership, etc. Nor are the usual ingredients of the dissident novel present: no mention of the Wall or of the shooting of escapees, no Stasi informers, no secret police visits at three in the morning; only the most distant reminiscences of the suave and smiling villains, familiar since Dostoevsky. No Big Brother; in short, none of the conventional trappings of literary totalitarianism, or of the pity and fear it is designed to arouse. The shortage of consumer goods, which looms so large in Western visions of Eastern unfreedom, is here simply a fact of life, as are the infuriating insolences of a bureaucracy identified by the West as the repressive state.

Of the dissidents themselves, heroically celebrated in the West, little trace is to be found until the final pages, when hitherto unfrequented preachers suddenly begin to attract followings—and to alter their language accordingly; samizdat groups spring up, organized around previously unknown or insignificant figures; massed crowds in the railway stations begin to impede traffic and the packed trains heading for the Czech and Hungarian borders begin to disrupt the protagonists' daily lives. Christian's hitherto apolitical mother becomes a demonstrator and would obviously be the heroine of an officially dissident novel; here, even the 'event' of her political conversion takes place offstage and never becomes part of the novel's narrative representation.

The ordeal of Christian himself—the youngest of the three protagonists and the one of whom it can be said that *Der Turm* is at least his *Bildungsroman*—thus remains the principal exhibit for a political—that is to say, an anti-communist—interpretation of this novel, which is certainly no apologia for socialism either. The regimentation of his military service (in this country, for all practical purposes it lasts six years!), his moment of revolt (at the accidental death of a fellow draftee) and his condemnation to hard labour—these experiences, which seem to have been at least partially autobiographical, are ambiguous to the degree to which they can also be accounted for by his rebellious temperament; not necessarily the best argument for political heroism. In any case, the oppressiveness of military service is no more unpleasant than what one finds in Western war novels, though no less, either; while Christian's labour in the mines (he will in fact eventually be reinstated in the army) gives the novelist a brief opportunity to convey the true proletarian underside of what remains an essentially bourgeois existence and indeed a privileged one at that.

Indeed, the very title of *Der Turm* designated a relatively affluent section of Dresden, whose spatial disposition—on an elevation reached by way of an antiquated funicular—and distinctive buildings play no small part in Tellkamp's story. The old saw, that this or that (generally non-Western) city is really a small world in which everyone—that is to say, the intelligentsia—knows everyone else, is certainly true of *Der Turm* and its narrative. (The inhabitants of the most important apartment houses are listed inside the back cover.) The novel is organized around three such inhabitants, related, but dwelling in different buildings: the teenager Christian; his father Richard, a hand surgeon with a short fuse but many high-placed contacts; and Christian's Uncle Meno, in some respects the central protagonist. A zoologist by training, he now occupies a significant position in a prestigious publishing house; which is to say that he is also professionally part of the state censorship system, even when he resists it.

Richard's dilemmas are the most familiar: he has to deal, in secret, with a second family (there is occasional half-hearted talk about 'fleeing' to the West). His position in the hospital is a vantage point from which we can observe the process of promotion in this system, as well as the ways in which hierarchy is felt in collegiality and in treatment. Richard's bluster is also capable of expressing itself in all kinds of aberrant adventures, from stealing a Christmas tree in a state-protected forest to the rebuilding in secret of a rare Hispano-Suiza car. These amount to a pushing of the envelope without serious consequences, since allowance has already been made for his character in his evaluation by the system. On the other hand, a series of futile attempts to appeal or at least to reduce his son's sentence testifies to the limits of influence of even so essential and valued a skilled professional. At least he escapes the fate of his superior, Dr Müller, a Party member and disciplinarian whom we first observe at Richard's birthday party, warning his colleagues (and Christian) against telling jokes against the regime. But Müller—head of the entire hospital system—has indulged himself privately in amassing an impressive (and expensive) collection of glass sculptures and artworks; on the day after his retirement he receives a summons to the police station and notification of a house search and confiscation of unlawful property. Müller destroys the collection before committing suicide, leaving a note whose final sentence reads: 'This is not the socialism we dreamed of'.

Richard is not, to be sure, unlike his other brother-in-law, a Party member; but it may still not be inappropriate to range him among a kind of cultural *Nomenklatura* (the Germans say *Bildungsbürgertum*, to distinguish them from the more secular garden-variety petty bourgeoisie); and to observe that, as is the case in so much of Lukács's 'critical realist' tradition, there is not much proletarian presence in this particular realism either. Still, one must note that as a hand surgeon, Richard's activity does lay a kind of manual labour in place; and his hobby of carpentry underscores a utopian handicraft tradition, explicitly related to the construction of *Dichtung*: 'As in the operating room here also [in his workshop] there reigned, not the speech of words, but rather that of the hands—a speech familiar to him, in which he felt at home'. In one of those lyric digressions which so frequently enrich and interrupt this lengthy novel, to our delight or annoyance, the hand itself is celebrated (the occasion is an operation on his own wife, injured after a domestic accident—or argument):

> He loved hands. Hands belonged to those living forms that gave him joy. He had studied hands: the lily-like femininity of Botticelli's women's fingers (and did these fingers not make up the hands themselves?); hands stubbornly convinced of something; hands in despair both about their failure to grow and their emergence from childhood; hands creamed and uncreamed; cooing hands, as unfathomable as moss; lady gardeners' tanned by the sap of plants,

and male stokers' so devoured by coal dust as to be unwashable . . . *Reading* hands had already given him satisfaction in his internship, challenges that might have seemed chafing or bothersome to others for him were sources of excitement, that you approached carefully and willingly, shyly, fearful of a nakedness that was however there, throbbing softly, in the lust to be known.

Richard's fascinations are here the very locus of a central ambiguity in praxis as such: they can express Sohn-Rethel's sense of the emergence of ideology from the split between manual and intellectual labour; or a phenomenon akin to those discoveries by Michael Fried, of the embodied auto-referentiality of the act of painting itself in the presence of the hand in a Menzel or a Caravaggio. And in fact this celebration of the 'hand' in *Der Turm* means both and faces both ways: as the shadow of a fundamental production process in this socialist state, in which it has slowly begun to deteriorate; and as the mirage of art and its objects and traditions, by which so many of its protagonists are mesmerized and, as it were, immobilized, under a timeless spell.

As for Christian, we have already observed that this otherwise unremarkable protagonist of the *Bildungsroman*—a shy, musically gifted boy, attentive to his uncle's lessons and experiencing the first bewildering approaches of love and sexuality, as well as the confusion of the unpolitical soul (this side inherited from his maternal uncle); reacting to the approach of the political with rebellious anger (his inheritance from his father)—this story is the place to which the representation of the peculiar oppressions of the DDR is centrally consigned.

But it is important to note that Christian's transgression is one of language, and that indeed, in this elitist version of DDR life and politics, it is language which is, from literature to politics, the crucial space in which the relationship to the state is tested: 'The problem is not what you did but what you said,' explains the interrogator to Christian. 'You damaged trust. This is not a matter of comrade junior officer Burre's death, which is of course regrettable. We will naturally investigate that, it goes without saying. But that's not the debate at present! That's a wholly different case. No, Hoffman, you and your buddy Kretschmar, whom we know very well, you made observations. You slandered us. You openly attacked our state.'

Our own first lesson in language sensitivity is in fact administered by the very same Dr Müller, who observes, at Richard's birthday party, 'Not a very good joke, gentlemen . . . we have responsibilities, gentlemen; and it is easy to take part in cheap denigrations of our country . . .' (the alternation between the words *Land* and *Staat* is a crucial clue; Müller here uses the former). Only the *Nomenklatura*, whose fidelity to the state can for the most part be taken for granted, are allowed to permit themselves the occasional political pleasantry, as we shall see. But as far as Christian is concerned, his lessons began much earlier, and in a rather surprising form:

> Erik Orré [an actor] had been a patient of Richard and wanted to show his thanks in an unusual way, namely to demonstrate the art of effective and professional lying to the boys, Richard estimating that this was something Christian in particular needed to learn; so the mime . . . practiced enthusiastic expressions of praise and flattery with them in front of a mirror, corrected their gestures, showed them how one could blush and grow pale at will, and how one could toady with dignity, emit stupidities with a straight face, using these as a mask over one's true thoughts, thresh out empty and yet intelligently flattering compliments, dissipate distrust in others and even in a pinch recognize other liars.

It is obviously not a lesson Christian has assimilated, despite his Uncle Meno's maxim: 'A wise man walks with his head down, almost invisible, like dust.'

Meno Rohde is by far the most interesting character in *Der Turm*, as well as being the most reserved; and despite the political ambiguity that has led a number of (West) German reviewers to charge him with the kind of apathy and submissiveness which not only kept the regime in power, but can even be read as a form of active support, by virtue of its very passivity. As the reader for Hermes–Verlag and its prestige series of classic authors, he is part and parcel of the censorship apparatus, as we have noted, however often he seems to argue against its decisions; and we may well wonder why it is always to his chapters that one looks forward and with his reticences and withdrawals that one feels sympathy. One of those rare people for whom silence is not shyness, nor indifference either, but rather some genuine distance from things, an almost Buddhist disengagement from personal action, coupled with an equally genuine passion and detached curiosity for observing it in others, Meno is a genuine intellectual—even though mostly patronized by the novel's official intellectuals, inasmuch as he is not a professional writer (save for his book reports and a private diary of which only the reader is given installments).

Yet there exists a more positive way of celebrating Meno's passivity and that is as scientific observation. His formation was in zoology, and it is this active detailing of the outside world and, in particular, of its life forms that Christian learns from his uncle, 'and is not troubled by Meno's demands, not angry when Meno in a friendly but implacable fashion gives him to understand that he had observed poorly and had not couched his impressions precisely enough in his language'. For it is also a training in *le mot juste*, in the fashion in which Flaubert corrected the descriptions and observations of the young Maupassant; and much of the ensuing discussion (in the passage just quoted) turns on the characterization of the kind of green to be identified on the wings of the Urania moth. (Veronese green? They finally settle on 'powder-green', which elicits not enthusiasm but the slightest nod of assent from his teacher.)

The professional hunt for bad punctuation and incorrect grammar in his authors' manuscripts therefore has its creative dimension in such observations, which are verbal as well as visual (let's also remember Nabokov's lepidopterology); but perhaps its social equivalent is something rather different. Meno himself observes a young writer, Judith Schevola, scrutinizing her fellows like 'a researcher on insects': 'her face distorted and twisted . . . only the eyes belonging to her . . . seeming to register everything with hostile curiosity.' But that drive is the motor impulse of great satire, as in Proust's portraits; and as for the smaller details, Meno's characterization might well come from the Thomas Mann of *Dr Faustus*: 'These are the orchestral parts to which the composer devoted his most painstaking labour, even though the public will scarcely hear them . . .'

It is to Meno then that we owe the most painstaking reconstruction of this seemingly timeless world, its antique objects rescued and stored up in the apartments of this once-prosperous quarter, the memory of the goods of yesteryear, marked with forgotten brand-names ('a Fortuna typewriter as bulky as an old "Konsum" cash-register', etc.). Sometimes indeed it seems as though the life-world of these characters were little more than one immense collection of pre-war objects and furniture, with the proviso that they are threatened at every moment by the coal-dust that also saturates this novel, by its odour when not by smears and coatings, or its literal omnipresence in Christian's life in the mines.

But it is to Meno also that we owe the extraordinary and well-nigh zoological tableau of the intellectual flora and fauna of the late DDR, in portraits in which German scholars and historians have identified historical DDR celebrities (not always known in the West). I will say a little about those portraits before returning in conclusion to the issue of temporality (or timelessness) of the Dresden of this novel. Nothing here is indeed quite so delicious as these portraits, whose mimicry—as in Proust—expresses malice and sympathy in equal parts. Here we truly have a kind of intellectual and artistic *Nomenklatura* of the regime, at one and the same time believers and cynics; and the central proving ground for *Der Turm*'s insistent foregrounding of language. Stalinist dandies, with their theatrical delight in outright affirmation: 'I was and remain an avowed defender of Stalin's order and have never concealed it . . . The murders were necessary, on the whole. Urgent times cannot have recourse to less-than-urgent measures. Desperate times cannot have recourse to less-than-desperate measures. The Soviet Union was surrounded, what else was he supposed to do?' Others are more resigned: 'We are a part of the Soviet Union, without it we couldn't exist [*waren nicht lebensfähig]'*. There are hatreds and passionate exchanges in the official meetings, particularly when exclusions are debated (that of Judith Schevola in particular); but the regional boss (Hans Modrow) deals with such decisions and the people they affect in a jovial yet matter-of-fact way. What goes without saying on this level—what the writers ought not to say in the first place—is rather different from the more standard ideological arguments of the everyday; as in the defence of the demands on professionals by Christian's girlfriend: 'This country gives you a free education and free healthcare, isn't that something? Don't you think we have to give something back?'

Characteristically, the sons of both *Nomenklatura* speakers above violently disagree with their positions, from the right and the left, respectively; thereby underscoring the generational dynamics that also runs through this novel. (Indeed, in my opinion, this theme is allegorical of socialism's most fundamental political problem, which is that of generational succession, or if you prefer the technical term, of social reproduction.) Still, it is important to realize that the apparent cynicism of this cultural *Nomenklatura*, at least in East Germany, in fact expresses a more complex psychological and political disposition, namely the tension between a believer's commitment to socialism and an insider's embarrassed distance from the Party's public decisions and rules (whose political necessity—the presence of the USSR—these intellectuals fully grasp). Irony is the expression of that embarrassment, and it is quite different from the cynicism of the characteristic West German talking points. I cannot resist quoting virtually the only sample of the latter (since these characters have so little contact with the West or indeed interest in it): this one we owe to a West German publisher visiting the Leipzig book fair, who in feigned astonishment at the continuing participation of the DDR writers in their state, places the following 'devastating' question: 'Would you be capable of killing a dolphin?'

Meno's presence in the novel then also affords an opening onto the question of temporality in what is, at least from one perspective, a lovingly detailed recreation of the space and objects, the daily life, of the DDR, with an intensity of feeling that might well be identified as nostalgia, or even *Ostalgie*—were it not for the obviously critical stance on the political administration of these realities, summed up in Christian's rash outburst after his accident: *'So was ist nur in diesem Scheissstaat möglich!'* To the degree to which the 'timelessness' of this moment of DDR history is identified as stagnation (*zastol*, in the Russian characterization of the Brezhnev years), and attributed to late socialism in general, the two perspectives are paradoxically one and the same.

On one level, to be sure, that of the *Bildungsroman*, the nostalgia is most easily explained as Christian's vision of his own childhood, brought abruptly to an end by military service. For Meno, the past is Dresden itself, virtually destroyed in the notorious firebombing of February 15, 1945: its geography, scarcely disguised by the cosmetic substitution of street names, the recognizable monuments and surviving buildings; even the very objects themselves which—as we have said and in the absence of investments in the production of consumer goods—resemble the artefacts in an immense museum of a past in which pre-war, Weimar and Wilhelminian Germany are virtually indistinguishable. Indeed, in this sense nostalgia is an unstable contagion, an existential contamination whose objects are interminably substitutable. So it is that the writing of a novel about the nostalgia of the people of the 1980s for some older world before the war becomes itself effortlessly transferable to the later years of the DDR in which that nostalgia was experienced.

Still, the seemingly timeless atmosphere of the first part of the novel—a timelessness which the title of Alexei Yurchak's study of the comparable period of Soviet history formulates as 'Everything was Forever until it was No More'—demands closer attention. The matter of consumer goods clearly enough marks a crucial objective misunderstanding and interference with Western perspectives on the situation, as when we experience traffic in Cuba as a delightful return to 1950s America, when it is in fact the result of the half-century-long blockade of the Communist island. Here, the seeming transformation of commodities into antiques may itself be taken as an allegory of a non-commodity-producing society, in which books, art works and musical instruments are cherished, and each rare item—the von Arbogasts' *Granatapfelsaft* from the Black Sea—is the object of heightened perception and intensified appreciation, as though the modernist 'make it new, make it strange' had been reversed in the direction of the past.

Meno's own peculiar 'ten-minute clock' might well be an example of this heightened perception, were it not for the fact that Richard's father had been an actual clock manufacturer, thus suggesting an older and more archaic state of production which we ourselves are tempted to confuse with handicraft work; and, above all, the fact that the novel is punctuated insistently by the tolling of bells, whose irreversible temporality itself foretells the impending intrusion of History into this seemingly arrested, timeless world. Yet timelessness is also a political issue in a different sense, and we may pause to observe the way in which so much of left politics today—unlike Marx's own passionate commitment to a streamlined technological future—seems to have adopted as its slogan Benjamin's odd idea that revolution means pulling the emergency brake on the runaway train of History, as though an admittedly runaway capitalism itself had the monopoly on change and futurity. It may well be that it is the gradual supersession of time by space in postmodernity which has released the very concept of temporality to a bewildering variety of speculative forms today. Thus Freud's notion of *Nachträglichkeit* (retroaction), in which the effect precedes the cause—a paradoxical, subordinate and pathological concept in its own period, governed by a now old-fashioned chronological time scheme—has become one of the dominant contenders for theoretical hegemony (in Lacan, Derrida and Deleuze alike); while older forms of succession associated with Hegel are dismissed as teleological.

But perhaps here too, in this experience of the East, some new lessons on time are available to us by way of the temporalities of *Der Turm*. Heiner Müller has characterized time in the DDR as a kind of waiting-room situation, in which the train is announced but never arrives—a novel version of the locomotive of History. As Charity Scribner noted in these pages in 1999: 'While the delays in the East allowed people to accumulate experience, Müller claims, the imperative to travel forward destroyed any such potential in the West.' This is another version of Benjamin's critique of progress, but perhaps it suggests some new possibilities for imagining what a different present of time and of history might look like.

At any rate, the temporality with which *Der Turm* concludes, and with which it represents the dissolution of the DDR, is not at all a heroic narrative of resistance and freedom. This is not, in other words, a political narrative at all: what we glimpse here is the breakdown of the infrastructure itself, rather than that of the political system. It is foreshadowed in Richard's experience of the power blackout in the hospital, and the desperate measures with which the staff attempt to keep the patients alive. In the heating crises, as well, in which the bitter cold of the German winter demands all kinds of black-market ingenuities. In the breakdown of the little funicular, which normally lifts the privileged inhabitants of the *Turm* suburb to their quaint dwellings. In the stalled railway stations of the city, finally, in which the whole transportation system of the region comes to a halt. This is, in other words, 'the material base' on which superstructural collapse is predicated; and appropriately it breaks into the characters' existential experience with all the intermittent confusion of unconscious causation generally, whether physical or mental.

Meanwhile, in an odd and somehow impersonal montage, these events and experiences in the late DDR present are juxtaposed and punctuated with what appear to be long extracts from a seemingly autobiographical narrative of World War Two and atrocities on the Eastern Front (presumably the work of the writer here named Altberg, but who seems to represent Franz Fühmann; on this interesting figure, see Benjamin Robinson's 2009 *The Skin of the System*). We have had very little information about the past of any of these characters—Richard's experience of the Dresden firebombing, for example, or Meno's involuntary change of profession. Now, suddenly, this historical disaster, as it were an East German Year Zero, seems to summon up overwhelming memories of the older one, in a flash flood of returning temporality. *Der Turm*, however, ends, as befits a novel whose main character is much concerned with punctuation, with a colon, leaving the whole matter of political futures very much open. The author has projected a sequel, about the year 1990, entitled *Lava*. Perhaps, as 1983 took five hundred pages of the present work, it will not be necessary to repeat that *tour de force* for this next even more interesting year. But one is certainly curious to learn the reactions to it of intellectuals and inner Party circles, as well as of Meno himself and his family.

John Hall, *Ernest Gellner: An Intellectual Biography*
Verso: London and New York 2010, £29.99, hardback
400 pp, 978 1 84467 602 6

Steven Lukes

THE GADFLY

Ernest Gellner died in Prague, the city of his childhood, in 1995, leaving a colossal intellectual legacy: some twenty books, two of them posthumous; a mass of articles, scholarly or journalistic, many of them provocative and polemical; all displaying his distinctive, scintillating intelligence. Gellner's range across topics and disciplines was remarkable and yet his thought displays considerable unity. Its foundations are most fully laid out in the second of the posthumous works, *Language and Solitude: Wittgenstein, Malinowski and the Habsburg Dilemma* (1998). Reconstructed from manuscripts by his son David, this is a work of synthesis: the closest Gellner came to an intellectual autobiography. It brings together philosophy, anthropology, and an interpretation of the Central European context of his upbringing, by juxtaposing the ideas of his lifelong *bête noire*, Wittgenstein, with those of Malinowski, a figure whom Gellner greatly admired, and whose work helped inspire his own turn from philosophy to anthropology.

The 'Habsburg Dilemma', according to Gellner, evoking their contrasting responses, amounted to a confrontation between atomists and organicists that 'meshes in with the alliances and hatreds of daily and political life'. The contrast was between what he called the 'atomic–universalist–individualist vision' and the 'communal–cultural vision'. He portrayed Wittgenstein as trapped within this opposition, veering unwittingly from one pole to the other. His early logical atomism expressed 'the solitude of the transcendental ego' seeking an account of 'what the world looks like to a solitary individual reflecting on the problem of how his mind, or language, can possibly "mean", i.e. reflect, the world'. By contrast, his later philosophy transplanted 'the populist idea of the authority of each distinctive culture to the problem of knowledge', concluding that 'mankind lives in cultural communities or, in [Wittgenstein's] words, "forms of life", which are self-sustaining, self-legitimating, logically and normatively final.' Malinowski, on the other hand, escaped the tyranny of this dichotomy; he was able to combine radical empiricism with a penchant for ethnographic fieldwork, a scientific approach to anthropology with a 'functionalist and romantic sense of the unity and interdependence of culture'. As for language, Malinowski allowed (though later mistakenly denied) that—though use-bound and context-linked—it properly strives in scientific and philosophical contexts to be context-free. And as for nationalism, he argued that the only hope was to 'limit the political power of nations, but permit, indeed enhance and encourage, the perpetuation of all those local cultures within which men have found their fulfilment and their freedom', thus 'depriving boundaries of some of their importance and symbolic potency'.

These positions came to be Gellner's own, as John Hall amply illustrates in this highly successful intellectual biography (although paradoxically *Language and Solitude* is one of the few works that Hall rather scants). Descended from secularized German-speaking Jews—his father had to learn Czech after the creation of the new Czechoslovak state—Gellner migrated to England in March 1939, at the age of thirteen. He went to school in St Albans and thence to Oxford, his degree interrupted by wartime service with the Czech Brigade besieging Dunkirk, and a brief, formative return to Prague under Soviet occupation. There followed a successful academic career, first briefly in Edinburgh, then for thirty-five years at the LSE, then to Cambridge and finally back to Prague in 1993. Gellner claimed to have benefited from his early life experiences. In an interview with John Davis he remarked that 'not having had a faith, I think I do understand . . . what Descartes and Hume and Kant were about, namely, the struggle to establish the foundations of knowledge', and '[n]ever having been a member of a community but having been on the margins of a number gave me an understanding of . . . what the yearning for community is all about.' And in a 'Reply to Critics' he recalled that from the Prague of his youth he had retained a memory of the difference between urban intellectuals and 'ideal man as conceived by the populist romanticism which was dominant in literature, art, even politics and philosophy', and that this had had considerable bearing on his decision to do fieldwork, and on his choice of location for the latter:

> When I first saw Berber villages of the central Atlas, each building clinging to the next, the style wholly homogeneous, the totality crying out that this was a *Gemeinschaft*, I knew at once that I wanted desperately to know, as far as an outsider ever could, what it was like *inside*.

It is clear that his life experience led him, as Perry Anderson observed, to a far less intense and exalted view of national allegiance than that of Max Weber, another figure who loomed large in his intellectual firmament. What Gellner favoured was the limited, liberal nationalism of Masaryk's Czechoslovak Republic, namely,

> the acceptance of 'forms of life,' from styles of food, handshakes and wallpapers to political rituals or personal relationships—but an acceptance which no longer endows anything with an aura of the absolute, but is ironic, tentative, optional, and above all discontinuous with serious knowledge and real conviction. In this limited sphere of 'culture,' relativism is indeed valid. In the sphere of serious conviction, on the other hand, relativism is not an option open to us *at all*.

Here we see Gellner's life-long commitment to an 'ethics of cognition' dedicated to 'the notion of culture-transcending truth', defended in his *Legitimation of Belief* (1974), according to which, as he wrote, 'all ideas, data, inquirers are equal, cognitive claims have to compete and confront data on terms of equality and they are not allowed to construct circular, self-confirming visions'. If we want to acquire 'powerful knowledge' we must, in Hall's words, 'act on the assumption that the world is regulated by cold, orderly, impersonal laws'. This view of legitimate knowledge, centring on science and its applications, excluding cognitive hierarchies and authorities (influenced by another figure he admired, Karl Popper), was the basis for Gellner's successive attacks across the years upon relativists, idealists, subjectivists, interpretivists, social constructionists, ethnomethodologists, postmodernists and other exponents of 'local knowledge', from Peter Winch to Clifford Geertz—inheritors all, he thought, of the errors of the later Wittgenstein, endorsers of locally prevailing commonsense. It also led him to be what Hall calls 'the scourge of re-enchantment theorists'. But admirable as it may be, this defence does raise a huge problem, namely that of values, which, Gellner concedes at the end of *Language and Solitude*, are 'instilled by contingent and variable cultures'. Are these not 'part of the sphere of serious conviction'? Is there not a problem here for the 'Enlightenment Fundamentalist Rationalism' that Gellner espoused in his *Postmodernism, Reason and Religion* (1992)? After all, the Enlightenment thinkers whom he held in high regard were universalists, one and all, about morals. And, as Hall remarks, 'the world of relative standards' was 'a world utterly unacceptable to Gellner.'

Hall's very considerable achievement is to have brought both Gellner and his ideas to life. He does the former by drawing upon a wide range of personal memories and interviews; archival materials, including a remarkable set of early aphorisms that Hall calls 'The Notes', and which prefigure later developments in Gellner's thinking; and, not least important, academic gossip. His treatment of Gellner's ideas is equally adept: the writings are discussed in sequence and placed in their intellectual contexts, Hall carefully reporting on—and frequently engaging robustly in—the controversies they have engendered, and documenting their reception. The ideas thereby come alive not so much through exposition (which tends to be elliptical) as in confrontation. It is a tribute to Hall's skill as an intellectual biographer, uniting empathy and critical distance, that Gellner's distinctive voice is present throughout—as are his failings and limitations.

Gellner's political outlook was, initially, liberal, social-democratic and, as he wrote to Anderson, 'deeply Philistine'. He was 'ready to pay the price of vulgarity for peace, reasonable diffused prosperity and equality. If God obliged me to choose for mankind, giving the option of living in a universalized Vienna of 1975 or 1905, I think I would, albeit with some private bitterness, be obliged to opt for 1975.' He became more conservative and tolerant of inequalities over the years (even, according to his daughter Sarah, enamoured of Margaret Thatcher), though not less liberal, reacting against post-1968 left intellectuals and later—and more anxiously and fearfully— against post-Soviet nationalism and Islamic fundamentalism. Hall records his dislike of hermeneutics, Marxism and Catholicism; the pillars, Gellner thought, of Charles Taylor's thought. But his attitude to Marxism was complex. He was impatient with what he saw as Western Marxists' idealist according of causal primacy to cultural factors, but was fascinated by, and supportive of, Soviet anthropologists' efforts to rescue Marxist theory by investigating transitions between modes of production. One significant dimension is almost entirely absent from Hall's account—namely Gellner's attitude towards, and views about, women. Except, that is, for one telling anecdote about his response, after many careful evasions, to an insistent line of feminist questioning at the American Anthropological Association about why he had paid no real attention to the role of women in historical development in his *Plough, Sword and Book* (1988). Hall writes that his 'penchant for speaking his mind—assuring the questioner that he liked women, but that they had nothing to do with historical development—caused mild uproar.'

Of his character the memories of friends and colleagues tell a consistent story. Ronald Dore, anxious on his arrival at the LSE, recalled that it was 'from Ernest that I learned not to give a damn about disciplinary tribes. He was a *franc tireur* of the disciplines, a zestful poacher who cocked a snook at all fences and gamekeepers.' His LSE colleague, David Glass, remarked that 'he did not know if the next revolution would come from the right or the left, but that Gellner would be the first to be shot in either case.' And Tom Nairn, a colleague in his last days in Prague, recalled him being 'irrepressible and in no way diminished, right to the end. Certainly conversations last year showed the same mixture of disrespect, malicious humour, deep insight and spiky, somewhat conservative, rectitude as twenty years before.' He loved, his biographer notes, to collect and retell jokes. Some of the best, I am convinced, he invented, such as the following. 'Have you heard the latest news about Bourdieu? He has decided to abolish the first syllable of his name.'

Gellner began his career as a philosopher but had already half-left the disciplinary tribe when he joined LSE's sociology department, from where, in turn, he became an anthropologist. His first, explosive entry into public view was with his *Words and Things: A Critical Account of Linguistic Philosophy and a Study in Ideology* (1959). This was a largely satirical denunciation of what he saw as the complacency of Oxford philosophers, deriving from the later Wittgenstein, 'dissolving' philosophical problems by appeal to 'ordinary language' usages and 'leaving everything as it is'; and their lack of curiosity about the world and the findings of the sciences. It was also an anthropological study, portraying them as 'the Narodniks of North Oxford', purveyors of 'a philosophic form eminently suitable for gentlemen.' The book was a *cause célèbre*. Bertrand Russell wrote a laudatory preface, Gilbert Ryle refused to have it reviewed in *Mind* and a flurry of philosophers responded to its charges in letters and reviews. (Another personal anecdote, for the record: I recall seeing *Jumpers*, Tom Stoppard's satirical play about academic philosophy, with Gellner and asking him what he thought of it. His response was: 'It's all publishable.').

Aside from the fun, Gellner developed a highly interesting argument in his essay on 'Concepts and Society', in contention with Winch and others, concerning the social function of conceptual ambiguity and contradiction, in which he cited the Berber concept of *baraka*. Gellner's central claim was that one must, as Hall writes, 'go beyond symbol and expression', assessing the world within from an external standpoint; and that it is 'the very falsity of certain beliefs' that 'makes possible an investigation into the ways in which they are sustained'. Hall argues that it was this insight that 'allowed him to become a brilliant sociologist of belief.' The two books *Thought and Change* (1964) and *Legitimation of Belief* (1974) are largely programmatic, rather caricatural works in which this assessment can be judged, the latter setting out the 'ethics of cognition' referred to above, through a bold 'mapping of modern epistemology'. It is, in my view, better vindicated in later applications, notably in his fine study *The Psychoanalytic Movement* (1985). Gellner also in these years took his distance from Michael Oakeshott's attack on rationalism and, far more fiercely, expressed his life-long contempt for Isaiah Berlin's style of thought, his view of Jewish identity and his value pluralism.

The turn to anthropology had come in 1953, with the doctoral research that would eventually become *Saints of the Atlas* (not published until 1969), pursued under the supervision of Raymond Firth. This lay at the origin of much of Gellner's later substantive work, deploying Evans-Pritchard's theory of segmentation and Ibn Khaldun's theory of the tribal circulation of elites—linking tribal solidarity and urban life. It incited his central interests in modernization and development, in constructing a model of Muslim society, and in nationalism. These last three concerns can indeed be seen as having generated his major substantive contributions, helpfully categorized by Hall in chapters respectively titled 'The Shape of History', 'The Sociology of Islam' and 'A General Theory of Nationalism'.

The key text for Gellner's account of modernization is his philosophy of history, *Plough, Sword and Book*. Most important here is his theory of the transition from *agraria* to *industria*—of the escape from a world where access to reality was as if from a 'multi-periscope submarine' to the modern world of standardized knowledge, graspable as if by 'jaws' (the rather awkward metaphors are Gellner's). There is—yet another metaphor—a 'big ditch' dividing the pre-modern from the modern. The book offers, in essence, a generalized Weberian account of the rise of the West. It posits, not any evolutionary logic but rather what Hall calls a 'curious concatenation of circumstances', of mutually shaping factors. Ideology played a decisive causal role, which took a benign form because pre-existing political pluralism restrained theocratic dreams, embraced toleration and encouraged the investigation of nature and economic growth. Cognitive power and its mass diffusion had a crucial part to play in this story, in which what Gellner called 'generic Protestantism', de-sacralizing the world, strongly encouraged scientific method by 'turning the orderly facts of its creation into the only evidence of its own design.' (The 'rigid and austere deity had no cognitive favourites and would not disclose its secrets capriciously to some.') This led to a mutual interaction of cognitive and economic growth. In marshalling the various criticisms and elaborations to which this account has been subject, Hall rather half-heartedly defends it against the charge of Eurocentrism —though it *is*, of course, Eurocentric—and focuses on what he calls its 'traces of Saint-Simonianism' and the influence of Raymond Aron—another pivotal figure for Gellner—that suggest 'a potential for modern industrialized society to stabilize, to find some point of rest'. But, Hall rightly argues, 'the modern world cannot be understood without recognizing the dynamics of capitalist society.' Gellner assumed that corporatist arrangements were always going to be available and, in general, his account—from which geopolitical factors are altogether absent—seriously underestimated the permanent instability of capitalist society.

Gellner's sociology of Islam, most fully set out in *Muslim Society* (1981), offered a model of Islamic civilization transcending the life of any particular state. The model incorporates Ibn Khaldun's theory of the circulation of elites and what Gellner called 'Hume's sociology of religion'—positing a perpetual pendulum swinging between enthusiastic monotheism and pluralist superstitions—and the anthropological theory of segmentation. Gellner thought that Islam had the capacity to provide an *ersatz* protestant ethic by 'unhinging the pendulum' and thus adapting itself to modernity, thereby resisting secularization. Focusing on its high tradition of law, literacy and discipline, his argument was that 'egalitarian scripturalism is more suited to a mobile technical society than ascriptive, mediationist, manipulative spiritual brokerage.' He envisaged Islam's survival in conditions of emulative industrialization, with scripturalism at its centre, sloughing off the peripheral styles as superstitions and unworthy accretions. Hall cites Patricia Crone's defence of the model as identifying a 'syndrome', manifested by 'the holy men of the tribal Middle East', which 'arises from the dispersal of power characteristic of segmentary organization.' But, first, how is this account to be squared with the 'big ditch' view, according to which science is necessary for economic growth? And, secondly, as Hall argues, Gellner plainly commits the double sin of over-generalizing and of essentializing modern Islam. It also, he further rightly claims, fails to account for the poor economic performance of many Muslim states because it excludes the impact of geopolitics and, indeed, of political factors in general.

It is, however, Gellner's 'general theory of nationalism', first and most clearly set out in *Thought and Change*, that is his most striking positive achievement. It is, indeed, a general theory and all the more vulnerable for that (a Popperian virtue Gellner welcomed). Nationalism, he claimed, arises under conditions of uneven development, when centralizing empires—'Megalomania'—alienate and humiliate linguistic minorities —'Ruritanians'—while seeking to modernize them, leading them to seek nation-states. Here is his most careful formulation:

> Political and economic forces, the aspirations of governments for greater power and of individuals for greater wealth, have in certain circumstances produced a world in which the division of labour is very advanced, the occupational structure highly unstable, and most work is semantic and communicative rather than physical. This situation in turn leads to the adoption of a standard and codified, literacy-linked ('High') idiom, requires business of all kinds to be conducted in its terms, and reduces persons who are not masters of that idiom (or not acceptable to its practitioners) to the status of humiliated second-class members, a condition from which one plausible and much-frequented escape route led through nationalist politics.

This formulation was intended by Gellner to show that his theory is genuinely causal and not functionalist, in the illicit form of proposing that needs generate what satisfies them—a charge to which he was often subjected and from which Hall largely and, I think, justifiably absolves him. He also shows how Gellner's account contrasts favourably with others, such as that of Elie Kedourie, with its focus on the decisive role of ideas, and that of Anthony Smith, for whom a primordial ethnic core is essential for a modern nation-state's success and viability. ('Some nations', Gellner wrote, playing on theological debates over the existence of Adam's *umbilicus*, 'have navels, some achieve navels, some have navels thrust upon them . . . it matters little. It is the need for navels engendered by modernity that matters.') Hall observes the central place that Gellner's theory occupies in the field of studies of nationalism but charges, once more, that it pays insufficient attention to geopolitical conflict and, most significantly, he adduces grounds for doubting Gellner's abiding assumption that cultural and linguistic homogeneity are necessary for societal success under modern conditions.

Hall concludes his book by reflecting on Gellner's response to the conflict between the demands of scientific rationality, which claimed his 'greatest allegiance', and the communitarian appeals of nationalism, which he sought to understand and explain: the Habsburg dilemma of *Language and Solitude*. He believed that the latter could and would be tamed as the logic of 'industrial society' unfolded but, at the end of his life, worried that this might not be so within the Islamic world. There can be no doubt about the continuing urgency and relevance of these questions. Through Hall's excellent book Ernest Gellner forces us to address them anew.